Mometrix
TEST PREPARATION

ABCTE

World History Exam Secrets Study Guide

DEAR FUTURE EXAM SUCCESS STORY

First of all, **THANK YOU** for purchasing Mometrix study materials!

Second, congratulations! You are one of the few determined test-takers who are committed to doing whatever it takes to excel on your exam. **You have come to the right place.** We developed these study materials with one goal in mind: to deliver you the information you need in a format that's concise and easy to use.

In addition to optimizing your guide for the content of the test, we've outlined our recommended steps for breaking down the preparation process into small, attainable goals so you can make sure you stay on track.

We've also analyzed the entire test-taking process, identifying the most common pitfalls and showing how you can overcome them and be ready for any curveball the test throws you.

Standardized testing is one of the biggest obstacles on your road to success, which only increases the importance of doing well in the high-pressure, high-stakes environment of test day. Your results on this test could have a significant impact on your future, and this guide provides the information and practical advice to help you achieve your full potential on test day.

Your success is our success

We would love to hear from you! If you would like to share the story of your exam success or if you have any questions or comments in regard to our products, please contact us at **800-673-8175** or **support@mometrix.com**.

Thanks again for your business and we wish you continued success!

Sincerely,
The Mometrix Test Preparation Team

Need more help? Check out our flashcards at:
http://MometrixFlashcards.com/ABCTE

Printed in the United States of America

TABLE OF CONTENTS

INTRODUCTION 1

SECRET KEY #1 – PLAN BIG, STUDY SMALL 2

SECRET KEY #2 – MAKE YOUR STUDYING COUNT 3

SECRET KEY #3 – PRACTICE THE RIGHT WAY 4

SECRET KEY #4 – PACE YOURSELF 6

SECRET KEY #5 – HAVE A PLAN FOR GUESSING 7

TEST-TAKING STRATEGIES 10

WORLD HISTORY PRE-1400 15

CHAPTER QUIZ 31

WORLD HISTORY 1400 TO 1914 32

CHAPTER QUIZ 45

WORLD HISTORY 1914 TO THE PRESENT 46

CHAPTER QUIZ 55

ABCTE WORLD HISTORY PRACTICE TEST 56

ANSWER KEY AND EXPLANATIONS 78

HOW TO OVERCOME TEST ANXIETY 89

ONLINE RESOURCES 95

Introduction

Thank you for purchasing this resource! You have made the choice to prepare yourself for a test that could have a huge impact on your future, and this guide is designed to help you be fully ready for test day. Obviously, it's important to have a solid understanding of the test material, but you also need to be prepared for the unique environment and stressors of the test, so that you can perform to the best of your abilities.

For this purpose, the first section that appears in this guide is the **Secret Keys**. We've devoted countless hours to meticulously researching what works and what doesn't, and we've boiled down our findings to the five most impactful steps you can take to improve your performance on the test. We start at the beginning with study planning and move through the preparation process, all the way to the testing strategies that will help you get the most out of what you know when you're finally sitting in front of the test.

We recommend that you start preparing for your test as far in advance as possible. However, if you've bought this guide as a last-minute study resource and only have a few days before your test, we recommend that you skip over the first two Secret Keys since they address a long-term study plan.

If you struggle with **test anxiety**, we strongly encourage you to check out our recommendations for how you can overcome it. Test anxiety is a formidable foe, but it can be beaten, and we want to make sure you have the tools you need to defeat it.

Secret Key #1 – Plan Big, Study Small

There's a lot riding on your performance. If you want to ace this test, you're going to need to keep your skills sharp and the material fresh in your mind. You need a plan that lets you review everything you need to know while still fitting in your schedule. We'll break this strategy down into three categories.

Information Organization

Start with the information you already have: the official test outline. From this, you can make a complete list of all the concepts you need to cover before the test. Organize these concepts into groups that can be studied together, and create a list of any related vocabulary you need to learn so you can brush up on any difficult terms. You'll want to keep this vocabulary list handy once you actually start studying since you may need to add to it along the way.

Time Management

Once you have your set of study concepts, decide how to spread them out over the time you have left before the test. Break your study plan into small, clear goals so you have a manageable task for each day and know exactly what you're doing. Then just focus on one small step at a time. When you manage your time this way, you don't need to spend hours at a time studying. Studying a small block of content for a short period each day helps you retain information better and avoid stressing over how much you have left to do. You can relax knowing that you have a plan to cover everything in time. In order for this strategy to be effective though, you have to start studying early and stick to your schedule. Avoid the exhaustion and futility that comes from last-minute cramming!

Study Environment

The environment you study in has a big impact on your learning. Studying in a coffee shop, while probably more enjoyable, is not likely to be as fruitful as studying in a quiet room. It's important to keep distractions to a minimum. You're only planning to study for a short block of time, so make the most of it. Don't pause to check your phone or get up to find a snack. It's also important to **avoid multitasking**. Research has consistently shown that multitasking will make your studying dramatically less effective. Your study area should also be comfortable and well-lit so you don't have the distraction of straining your eyes or sitting on an uncomfortable chair.

The time of day you study is also important. You want to be rested and alert. Don't wait until just before bedtime. Study when you'll be most likely to comprehend and remember. Even better, if you know what time of day your test will be, set that time aside for study. That way your brain will be used to working on that subject at that specific time and you'll have a better chance of recalling information.

Finally, it can be helpful to team up with others who are studying for the same test. Your actual studying should be done in as isolated an environment as possible, but the work of organizing the information and setting up the study plan can be divided up. In between study sessions, you can discuss with your teammates the concepts that you're all studying and quiz each other on the details. Just be sure that your teammates are as serious about the test as you are. If you find that your study time is being replaced with social time, you might need to find a new team.

Secret Key #2 – Make Your Studying Count

You're devoting a lot of time and effort to preparing for this test, so you want to be absolutely certain it will pay off. This means doing more than just reading the content and hoping you can remember it on test day. It's important to make every minute of study count. There are two main areas you can focus on to make your studying count.

Retention

It doesn't matter how much time you study if you can't remember the material. You need to make sure you are retaining the concepts. To check your retention of the information you're learning, try recalling it at later times with minimal prompting. Try carrying around flashcards and glance at one or two from time to time or ask a friend who's also studying for the test to quiz you.

To enhance your retention, look for ways to put the information into practice so that you can apply it rather than simply recalling it. If you're using the information in practical ways, it will be much easier to remember. Similarly, it helps to solidify a concept in your mind if you're not only reading it to yourself but also explaining it to someone else. Ask a friend to let you teach them about a concept you're a little shaky on (or speak aloud to an imaginary audience if necessary). As you try to summarize, define, give examples, and answer your friend's questions, you'll understand the concepts better and they will stay with you longer. Finally, step back for a big picture view and ask yourself how each piece of information fits with the whole subject. When you link the different concepts together and see them working together as a whole, it's easier to remember the individual components.

Finally, practice showing your work on any multi-step problems, even if you're just studying. Writing out each step you take to solve a problem will help solidify the process in your mind, and you'll be more likely to remember it during the test.

Modality

Modality simply refers to the means or method by which you study. Choosing a study modality that fits your own individual learning style is crucial. No two people learn best in exactly the same way, so it's important to know your strengths and use them to your advantage.

For example, if you learn best by visualization, focus on visualizing a concept in your mind and draw an image or a diagram. Try color-coding your notes, illustrating them, or creating symbols that will trigger your mind to recall a learned concept. If you learn best by hearing or discussing information, find a study partner who learns the same way or read aloud to yourself. Think about how to put the information in your own words. Imagine that you are giving a lecture on the topic and record yourself so you can listen to it later.

For any learning style, flashcards can be helpful. Organize the information so you can take advantage of spare moments to review. Underline key words or phrases. Use different colors for different categories. Mnemonic devices (such as creating a short list in which every item starts with the same letter) can also help with retention. Find what works best for you and use it to store the information in your mind most effectively and easily.

Secret Key #3 – Practice the Right Way

Your success on test day depends not only on how many hours you put into preparing, but also on whether you prepared the right way. It's good to check along the way to see if your studying is paying off. One of the most effective ways to do this is by taking practice tests to evaluate your progress. Practice tests are useful because they show exactly where you need to improve. Every time you take a practice test, pay special attention to these three groups of questions:

- The questions you got wrong
- The questions you had to guess on, even if you guessed right
- The questions you found difficult or slow to work through

This will show you exactly what your weak areas are, and where you need to devote more study time. Ask yourself why each of these questions gave you trouble. Was it because you didn't understand the material? Was it because you didn't remember the vocabulary? Do you need more repetitions on this type of question to build speed and confidence? Dig into those questions and figure out how you can strengthen your weak areas as you go back to review the material.

Additionally, many practice tests have a section explaining the answer choices. It can be tempting to read the explanation and think that you now have a good understanding of the concept. However, an explanation likely only covers part of the question's broader context. Even if the explanation makes perfect sense, **go back and investigate** every concept related to the question until you're positive you have a thorough understanding.

As you go along, keep in mind that the practice test is just that: practice. Memorizing these questions and answers will not be very helpful on the actual test because it is unlikely to have any of the same exact questions. If you only know the right answers to the sample questions, you won't be prepared for the real thing. **Study the concepts** until you understand them fully, and then you'll be able to answer any question that shows up on the test.

It's important to wait on the practice tests until you're ready. If you take a test on your first day of study, you may be overwhelmed by the amount of material covered and how much you need to learn. Work up to it gradually.

On test day, you'll need to be prepared for answering questions, managing your time, and using the test-taking strategies you've learned. It's a lot to balance, like a mental marathon that will have a big impact on your future. Like training for a marathon, you'll need to start slowly and work your way up. When test day arrives, you'll be ready.

Start with the strategies you've read in the first two Secret Keys—plan your course and study in the way that works best for you. If you have time, consider using multiple study resources to get different approaches to the same concepts. It can be helpful to see difficult concepts from more than one angle. Then find a good source for practice tests. Many times, the test website will suggest potential study resources or provide sample tests.

Practice Test Strategy

If you're able to find at least three practice tests, we recommend this strategy:

Untimed and Open-Book Practice

Take the first test with no time constraints and with your notes and study guide handy. Take your time and focus on applying the strategies you've learned.

Timed and Open-Book Practice

Take the second practice test open-book as well, but set a timer and practice pacing yourself to finish in time.

Timed and Closed-Book Practice

Take any other practice tests as if it were test day. Set a timer and put away your study materials. Sit at a table or desk in a quiet room, imagine yourself at the testing center, and answer questions as quickly and accurately as possible.

Keep repeating timed and closed-book tests on a regular basis until you run out of practice tests or it's time for the actual test. Your mind will be ready for the schedule and stress of test day, and you'll be able to focus on recalling the material you've learned.

Secret Key #4 – Pace Yourself

Once you're fully prepared for the material on the test, your biggest challenge on test day will be managing your time. Just knowing that the clock is ticking can make you panic even if you have plenty of time left. Work on pacing yourself so you can build confidence against the time constraints of the exam. Pacing is a difficult skill to master, especially in a high-pressure environment, so **practice is vital**.

Set time expectations for your pace based on how much time is available. For example, if a section has 60 questions and the time limit is 30 minutes, you know you have to average 30 seconds or less per question in order to answer them all. Although 30 seconds is the hard limit, set 25 seconds per question as your goal, so you reserve extra time to spend on harder questions. When you budget extra time for the harder questions, you no longer have any reason to stress when those questions take longer to answer.

Don't let this time expectation distract you from working through the test at a calm, steady pace, but keep it in mind so you don't spend too much time on any one question. Recognize that taking extra time on one question you don't understand may keep you from answering two that you do understand later in the test. If your time limit for a question is up and you're still not sure of the answer, mark it and move on, and come back to it later if the time and the test format allow. If the testing format doesn't allow you to return to earlier questions, just make an educated guess; then put it out of your mind and move on.

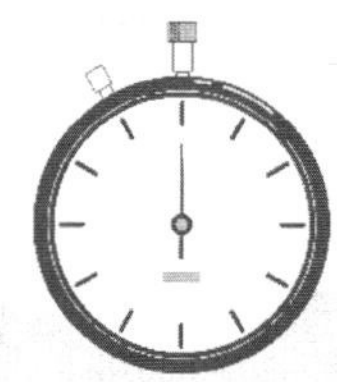

On the easier questions, be careful not to rush. It may seem wise to hurry through them so you have more time for the challenging ones, but it's not worth missing one if you know the concept and just didn't take the time to read the question fully. Work efficiently but make sure you understand the question and have looked at all of the answer choices, since more than one may seem right at first.

Even if you're paying attention to the time, you may find yourself a little behind at some point. You should speed up to get back on track, but do so wisely. Don't panic; just take a few seconds less on each question until you're caught up. Don't guess without thinking, but do look through the answer choices and eliminate any you know are wrong. If you can get down to two choices, it is often worthwhile to guess from those. Once you've chosen an answer, move on and don't dwell on any that you skipped or had to hurry through. If a question was taking too long, chances are it was one of the harder ones, so you weren't as likely to get it right anyway.

On the other hand, if you find yourself getting ahead of schedule, it may be beneficial to slow down a little. The more quickly you work, the more likely you are to make a careless mistake that will affect your score. You've budgeted time for each question, so don't be afraid to spend that time. Practice an efficient but careful pace to get the most out of the time you have.

Secret Key #5 – Have a Plan for Guessing

When you're taking the test, you may find yourself stuck on a question. Some of the answer choices seem better than others, but you don't see the one answer choice that is obviously correct. What do you do?

The scenario described above is very common, yet most test takers have not effectively prepared for it. Developing and practicing a plan for guessing may be one of the single most effective uses of your time as you get ready for the exam.

In developing your plan for guessing, there are three questions to address:

- When should you start the guessing process?
- How should you narrow down the choices?
- Which answer should you choose?

When to Start the Guessing Process

Unless your plan for guessing is to select C every time (which, despite its merits, is not what we recommend), you need to leave yourself enough time to apply your answer elimination strategies. Since you have a limited amount of time for each question, that means that if you're going to give yourself the best shot at guessing correctly, you have to decide quickly whether or not you will guess.

Of course, the best-case scenario is that you don't have to guess at all, so first, see if you can answer the question based on your knowledge of the subject and basic reasoning skills. Focus on the key words in the question and try to jog your memory of related topics. Give yourself a chance to bring the knowledge to mind, but once you realize that you don't have (or you can't access) the knowledge you need to answer the question, it's time to start the guessing process.

It's almost always better to start the guessing process too early than too late. It only takes a few seconds to remember something and answer the question from knowledge. Carefully eliminating wrong answer choices takes longer. Plus, going through the process of eliminating answer choices can actually help jog your memory.

Summary: Start the guessing process as soon as you decide that you can't answer the question based on your knowledge.

How to Narrow Down the Choices

The next chapter in this book (**Test-Taking Strategies**) includes a wide range of strategies for how to approach questions and how to look for answer choices to eliminate. You will definitely want to read those carefully, practice them, and figure out which ones work best for you. Here though, we're going to address a mindset rather than a particular strategy.

Your odds of guessing an answer correctly depend on how many options you are choosing from.

Number of options left	5	4	3	2	1
Odds of guessing correctly	20%	25%	33%	50%	100%

You can see from this chart just how valuable it is to be able to eliminate incorrect answers and make an educated guess, but there are two things that many test takers do that cause them to miss out on the benefits of guessing:

- Accidentally eliminating the correct answer
- Selecting an answer based on an impression

We'll look at the first one here, and the second one in the next section.

To avoid accidentally eliminating the correct answer, we recommend a thought exercise called **the $5 challenge**. In this challenge, you only eliminate an answer choice from contention if you are willing to bet $5 on it being wrong. Why $5? Five dollars is a small but not insignificant amount of money. It's an amount you could afford to lose but wouldn't want to throw away. And while losing $5 once might not hurt too much, doing it twenty times will set you back $100. In the same way, each small decision you make—eliminating a choice here, guessing on a question there—won't by itself impact your score very much, but when you put them all together, they can make a big difference. By holding each answer choice elimination decision to a higher standard, you can reduce the risk of accidentally eliminating the correct answer.

The $5 challenge can also be applied in a positive sense: If you are willing to bet $5 that an answer choice *is* correct, go ahead and mark it as correct.

Summary: Only eliminate an answer choice if you are willing to bet $5 that it is wrong.

Which Answer to Choose

You're taking the test. You've run into a hard question and decided you'll have to guess. You've eliminated all the answer choices you're willing to bet $5 on. Now you have to pick an answer. Why do we even need to talk about this? Why can't you just pick whichever one you feel like when the time comes?

The answer to these questions is that if you don't come into the test with a plan, you'll rely on your impression to select an answer choice, and if you do that, you risk falling into a trap. The test writers know that everyone who takes their test will be guessing on some of the questions, so they intentionally write wrong answer choices to seem plausible. You still have to pick an answer though, and if the wrong answer choices are designed to look right, how can you ever be sure that you're not falling for their trap? The best solution we've found to this dilemma is to take the decision out of your hands entirely. Here is the process we recommend:

Once you've eliminated any choices that you are confident (willing to bet $5) are wrong, select the first remaining choice as your answer.

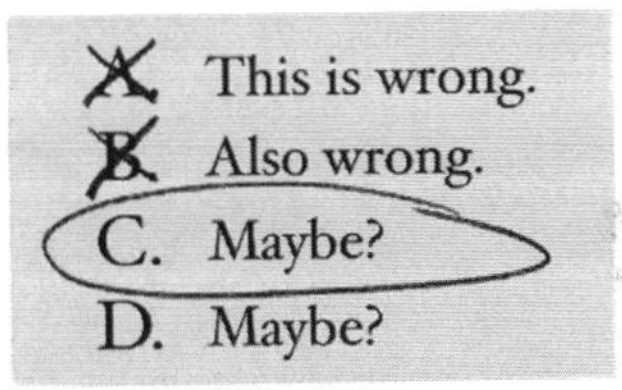

Whether you choose to select the first remaining choice, the second, or the last, the important thing is that you use some preselected standard. Using this approach guarantees that you will not be enticed into selecting an answer choice that looks right, because you are not basing your decision on how the answer choices look.

This is not meant to make you question your knowledge. Instead, it is to help you recognize the difference between your knowledge and your impressions. There's a huge difference between thinking an answer is right because of what you know, and thinking an answer is right because it looks or sounds like it should be right.

Summary: To ensure that your selection is appropriately random, make a predetermined selection from among all answer choices you have not eliminated.

Test-Taking Strategies

This section contains a list of test-taking strategies that you may find helpful as you work through the test. By taking what you know and applying logical thought, you can maximize your chances of answering any question correctly!

It is very important to realize that every question is different and every person is different: no single strategy will work on every question, and no single strategy will work for every person. That's why we've included all of them here, so you can try them out and determine which ones work best for different types of questions and which ones work best for you.

Question Strategies

✓ Read Carefully

Read the question and the answer choices carefully. Don't miss the question because you misread the terms. You have plenty of time to read each question thoroughly and make sure you understand what is being asked. Yet a happy medium must be attained, so don't waste too much time. You must read carefully and efficiently.

✓ Contextual Clues

Look for contextual clues. If the question includes a word you are not familiar with, look at the immediate context for some indication of what the word might mean. Contextual clues can often give you all the information you need to decipher the meaning of an unfamiliar word. Even if you can't determine the meaning, you may be able to narrow down the possibilities enough to make a solid guess at the answer to the question.

✓ Prefixes

If you're having trouble with a word in the question or answer choices, try dissecting it. Take advantage of every clue that the word might include. Prefixes can be a huge help. Usually, they allow you to determine a basic meaning. *Pre-* means before, *post-* means after, *pro-* is positive, *de-* is negative. From prefixes, you can get an idea of the general meaning of the word and try to put it into context.

✓ Hedge Words

Watch out for critical hedge words, such as *likely, may, can, often, almost, mostly, usually, generally, rarely,* and *sometimes*. Question writers insert these hedge phrases to cover every possibility. Often an answer choice will be wrong simply because it leaves no room for exception. Be on guard for answer choices that have definitive words such as *exactly* and *always*.

✓ Switchback Words

Stay alert for *switchbacks*. These are the words and phrases frequently used to alert you to shifts in thought. The most common switchback words are *but, although,* and *however*. Others include *nevertheless, on the other hand, even though, while, in spite of, despite,* and *regardless of*. Switchback words are important to catch because they can change the direction of the question or an answer choice.

⊘ Face Value

When in doubt, use common sense. Accept the situation in the problem at face value. Don't read too much into it. These problems will not require you to make wild assumptions. If you have to go beyond creativity and warp time or space in order to have an answer choice fit the question, then you should move on and consider the other answer choices. These are normal problems rooted in reality. The applicable relationship or explanation may not be readily apparent, but it is there for you to figure out. Use your common sense to interpret anything that isn't clear.

Answer Choice Strategies

⊘ Answer Selection

The most thorough way to pick an answer choice is to identify and eliminate wrong answers until only one is left, then confirm it is the correct answer. Sometimes an answer choice may immediately seem right, but be careful. The test writers will usually put more than one reasonable answer choice on each question, so take a second to read all of them and make sure that the other choices are not equally obvious. As long as you have time left, it is better to read every answer choice than to pick the first one that looks right without checking the others.

⊘ Answer Choice Families

An answer choice family consists of two (in rare cases, three) answer choices that are very similar in construction and cannot all be true at the same time. If you see two answer choices that are direct opposites or parallels, one of them is usually the correct answer. For instance, if one answer choice says that quantity *x* increases and another either says that quantity *x* decreases (opposite) or says that quantity *y* increases (parallel), then those answer choices would fall into the same family. An answer choice that doesn't match the construction of the answer choice family is more likely to be incorrect. Most questions will not have answer choice families, but when they do appear, you should be prepared to recognize them.

⊘ Eliminate Answers

Eliminate answer choices as soon as you realize they are wrong, but make sure you consider all possibilities. If you are eliminating answer choices and realize that the last one you are left with is also wrong, don't panic. Start over and consider each choice again. There may be something you missed the first time that you will realize on the second pass.

⊘ Avoid Fact Traps

Don't be distracted by an answer choice that is factually true but doesn't answer the question. You are looking for the choice that answers the question. Stay focused on what the question is asking for so you don't accidentally pick an answer that is true but incorrect. Always go back to the question and make sure the answer choice you've selected actually answers the question and is not merely a true statement.

⊘ Extreme Statements

In general, you should avoid answers that put forth extreme actions as standard practice or proclaim controversial ideas as established fact. An answer choice that states the "process should be used in certain situations, if..." is much more likely to be correct than one that states the "process should be discontinued completely." The first is a calm rational statement and doesn't even make a definitive, uncompromising stance, using a hedge word *if* to provide wiggle room, whereas the second choice is far more extreme.

⊘ Benchmark

As you read through the answer choices and you come across one that seems to answer the question well, mentally select that answer choice. This is not your final answer, but it's the one that will help you evaluate the other answer choices. The one that you selected is your benchmark or standard for judging each of the other answer choices. Every other answer choice must be compared to your benchmark. That choice is correct until proven otherwise by another answer choice beating it. If you find a better answer, then that one becomes your new benchmark. Once you've decided that no other choice answers the question as well as your benchmark, you have your final answer.

⊘ Predict the Answer

Before you even start looking at the answer choices, it is often best to try to predict the answer. When you come up with the answer on your own, it is easier to avoid distractions and traps because you will know exactly what to look for. The right answer choice is unlikely to be word-for-word what you came up with, but it should be a close match. Even if you are confident that you have the right answer, you should still take the time to read each option before moving on.

General Strategies

⊘ Tough Questions

If you are stumped on a problem or it appears too hard or too difficult, don't waste time. Move on! Remember though, if you can quickly check for obviously incorrect answer choices, your chances of guessing correctly are greatly improved. Before you completely give up, at least try to knock out a couple of possible answers. Eliminate what you can and then guess at the remaining answer choices before moving on.

⊘ Check Your Work

Since you will probably not know every term listed and the answer to every question, it is important that you get credit for the ones that you do know. Don't miss any questions through careless mistakes. If at all possible, try to take a second to look back over your answer selection and make sure you've selected the correct answer choice and haven't made a costly careless mistake (such as marking an answer choice that you didn't mean to mark). This quick double check should more than pay for itself in caught mistakes for the time it costs.

⊘ Pace Yourself

It's easy to be overwhelmed when you're looking at a page full of questions; your mind is confused and full of random thoughts, and the clock is ticking down faster than you would like. Calm down and maintain the pace that you have set for yourself. Especially as you get down to the last few minutes of the test, don't let the small numbers on the clock make you panic. As long as you are on track by monitoring your pace, you are guaranteed to have time for each question.

⊘ Don't Rush

It is very easy to make errors when you are in a hurry. Maintaining a fast pace in answering questions is pointless if it makes you miss questions that you would have gotten right otherwise. Test writers like to include distracting information and wrong answers that seem right. Taking a little extra time to avoid careless mistakes can make all the difference in your test score. Find a pace that allows you to be confident in the answers that you select.

⊘ Keep Moving

Panicking will not help you pass the test, so do your best to stay calm and keep moving. Taking deep breaths and going through the answer elimination steps you practiced can help to break through a stress barrier and keep your pace.

Final Notes

The combination of a solid foundation of content knowledge and the confidence that comes from practicing your plan for applying that knowledge is the key to maximizing your performance on test day. As your foundation of content knowledge is built up and strengthened, you'll find that the strategies included in this chapter become more and more effective in helping you quickly sift through the distractions and traps of the test to isolate the correct answer.

Now that you're preparing to move forward into the test content chapters of this book, be sure to keep your goal in mind. As you read, think about how you will be able to apply this information on the test. If you've already seen sample questions for the test and you have an idea of the question format and style, try to come up with questions of your own that you can answer based on what you're reading. This will give you valuable practice applying your knowledge in the same ways you can expect to on test day.

Good luck and good studying!

World History Pre-1400

Lower Paleolithic Period

The **Paleolithic period** is the earliest period of human development, as well as the longest. It is also commonly referred to as the **Old Stone Age**. It lasted from about 2.5 million years ago until about 300,000 years ago. Development during this period was excruciatingly slow. The Paleolithic period is usually divided into three sections: the Lower, Middle, and Upper. The **Lower Paleolithic period** is characterized by the appearance of stone tools; the chopping tools found at the Olduvai Gorge in Tanzania are from this period and date back over a million years. They were probably made by **Australopithecus**, an ancestor of modern humans. Anthropologists have also found stone tools believed to have been made by Homo erectus between 100,000 and 500,000 years ago.

Middle and Upper Paleolithic Periods

The Middle Paleolithic period occurred about 300,000 years ago until about 40,000 years ago. During this time, the Mousterian culture of Neanderthal men was active in Europe, North Africa, Palestine, and Siberia. These ancestors of modern man lived in caves and had the use of fire. They hunted prehistoric mammals and had slightly more sophisticated tools than their forebears, including crude needles for sewing furs together. These people may have practiced some sort of religion. In the **Upper Paleolithic** period, about 40,000 years ago until about 10,000 years ago, Neanderthals were replaced by varieties of Homo sapiens, including Cro-Magnon man and Grimaldi man. A number of diverse cultures flourished during this period, and the first manmade shelters arose. This was also the period in which people first crafted jewelry and illustrated drawings on the walls of caves.

Solutrean and Magdalenian Phase of the Paleolithic Period

During the **Upper Paleolithic period**, hunters entered Europe from the east and conquered the more primitive cultures living there. These victorious hunters were known as the **Solutreans**. These people are noted for their fine spearheads, which they used to hunt wild horses. The Solutreans were, in turn, replaced by the **Magdalenians**, the most advanced phase of the Paleolithic period. The Magdalenians subsisted mainly through fishing and reindeer hunting. They developed extremely precise tools and sophisticated weapons, such as the atlatl, a device that made it possible to throw a spear over a great distance. Most of all, though, the Magdalenians are known for their cave paintings in modern-day France.

Mesolithic Period

The Mesolithic period, otherwise known as the **Middle Stone Age**, began roughly 10,000 years ago and ended with the introduction of farming (dates vary by culture). In some areas, the use of farming was already beginning at the end of the Paleolithic era, and therefore there may not be a true **Mesolithic period**. The most extensive examples of this kind of culture are found in Northern Europe, where the end of the **Ice Age** created much greater changes in the ability to live off of the land. The remains of the Mesolithic period are mainly just middens (rubbish heaps), as well as some deforestation. The people of the Mesolithic period made small tools out of flint; fishing tackle, canoes, and bows have been found at some sites.

Neolithic Period

The Neolithic period, also known as the **New Stone Age**, refers to that stage of human cultural evolution in which man developed stone tools, settled in villages, and began making crafts. In order to begin living in towns, man had to learn how to domesticate animals and sustain agriculture;

formerly, in the Paleolithic and Mesolithic periods, man had subsisted through hunting, fishing, and gathering. The **Neolithic period** is said to have ended when urban civilizations began, or when metal tools or writing began. Because the designation of Neolithic depends on these factors, anthropologists date its occurrence differently for different regions and populations. At present, anthropologists believe that the earliest Neolithic culture was in southwest Asia between 8000 and 6000 BC.

Spread of Neolithic Culture

Most anthropologists date the beginning of **Neolithic culture** at somewhere between 8000 and 6000 BC. It began with the domestication of plants (wheat, barley, and millet) and animals (cattle, sheep, and goats). The Neolithic culture in the valley between the Tigris and Euphrates Rivers gradually evolved into a more urban civilization by 3500 BC. Meanwhile, Neolithic cultural advances spread through Europe, the Nile Valley, the Indus Valley, and the Huang He Valley. In these regions, the innovations of the Neolithic period were intermixed with the particulars of the region; in the Huang He region, for instance, rice cultivation was a product of advances in agriculture. By 1500 BC, Neolithic culture had spread to Mexico and South America. In these areas, corn, beans, and squash were the major crops.

Sumerians of Mesopotamia

Mesopotamia, the region between the Tigris and Euphrates Rivers in what is now considered the Middle East, contained several different early civilizations of which the **Sumerians** were one of the more prominent. They developed the system of writing known as **cuneiform**, by which they elaborated their theories on mathematics and astronomy. The Sumerians also had a detailed system of **laws** and traded widely with other groups throughout the region. They even traded with civilizations as far away as Egypt and India. There was no coin or currency system at this time, thus trade was conducted on the barter system, in which goods are exchanged for one another, directly.

Babylonian Civilization of Mesopotamia

After the Sumerian civilization declined, the next dominant civilization was **Babylon**. The Babylonians conquered the Sumerians and established a city on the Euphrates River in approximately 1,750 B.C. One of the most famous Babylonian rulers was **Hammurabi**, who established the famous **Code of Hammurabi**, an extremely detailed set of laws. This marked the first time that a set of rules governing every aspect of social life was applied to an entire people. The Babylonians are also known for their construction of **ziggurats**, long pyramid-like structures that were used as religious temples. Over time, the Babylonians acquired a reputation as a sensuous and hedonistic people, and the name Babylon has come to stand for any debauched civilization.

Review Video: Early Mesopotamia: The Babylonians
Visit mometrix.com/academy and enter code: 340325

Review Video: Early Mesopotamia: The Sumerians
Visit mometrix.com/academy and enter code: 939880

Pyramids of Egypt

The incredible engineering skills of the Egyptians are most famously displayed in the **pyramids** clustered along the Nile River. These were built roughly between 2700 and 2500 BC. The largest of the structures, the **Khufu pyramid** at Giza, is estimated to have taken 20 years and 100,000 laborers to construct. Today, it stands at 450 feet; some of its height has been lost to erosion. These pyramids were built as burial sites for the pharaohs, who were believed to continue their rule in the afterlife. Peasants worked on the pyramids in exchange for food and shelter. The shape of the pyramids was meant to symbolize the slanting rays of the sun, with sloping sides meant to help the ka (soul) of the pharaoh climb to the sky and join the gods.

Review Video: Ancient Egypt
Visit mometrix.com/academy and enter code: 398041

Religion in Africa

Sub-Saharan Africa was composed of disparate tribes. Most of Africa practiced **animistic religion**, in which it is believed that deities are embodied in the animals that people depend upon for food and service. Ritual and participatory worship were important; common activities included drumming, dancing, divination, and sacrifices. These religions typically had well-developed concepts of good and evil; they believed that some evil, disasters, and illnesses were produced by witchcraft, and that specialists (known as diviners) were required to combat the power of these malevolent beings. Many African peoples shared an underlying belief in a **creator deity**, whose power was expressed through the **ancestors** who founded the tribe. These deceased ancestors were a link between the living and the deities. African tribal religions showed a remarkable resilience when they began to come into contact with monotheistic religions.

Indus Valley Civilizations

The **Indus River Valley** is an area bordered by the Himalayan Mountains in what is now Pakistan. The people of this region developed a system of writing, as well as systems of weight and measurement which were useful in trade. They exchanged goods with the people of Mesopotamia in the west, as well as with the people of Tibet in the east. The Aryans invaded this region and brought with them iron technology and the Sanskrit language. The introduction of iron tools made it possible to cultivate the forests of the **Ganges River Valley** in what is now India.

Early Cities of Mohenjo-Daro and Harappa in the Indus Valley

Both the Indus Valley and Egyptian civilizations featured extremely well-planned **cities**. In the Indus Valley, the cities of **Mohenjo-Daro** and **Harappa** were located along the Indus River, in what is now Pakistan. Each of these cities was built around 2500 BC and housed approximately 30,000 citizens. They were each designed in a grid-like pattern, with streets running east-west and north-south. Both Mohenjo-Daro and Harrapa had bathhouses, sewer systems, and organized garbage collection. The structures in these cities were built with oven-fired bricks, which made them durable. Unlike in Egypt, where technological advances were used to enhance religious practice, the people of the Indus Valley used their technology to improve sanitation.

Earliest Civilization in What Would Become China

The earliest civilizations in what would become China flourished along the banks of the **Huang He (Yellow) River** before the year 2000 BC. The first Chinese dynasty was the **Xia** (Hsia), succeeded by the **Shang** dynasty. In this period, the rulers established an intricate system of government and a comprehensive judiciary. The basic components of this system would be preserved in Chinese civilization for centuries. The distinctive Chinese style of writing also developed during this period. Like Egyptian hieroglyphs, the Chinese pictographs were meant to resemble their definition. Over time, though, the Chinese characters have come to resemble their definitions less and less.

Zhou Dynasty

The Zhou dynasty, which ran from roughly 1030 to 221 BC, is generally considered to be the third Chinese dynasty, after the Shang. The **Zhou** were brought into power by the commander **Wu**, who declared that the decadent Shang monarchs had forfeited the mandate of heaven (in other words, God's approval of their reign). The Zhou dynasty is generally divided into two parts: The **Western**

Zhou ran a feudal-type state in the central plain and the area around the Yellow River. The later **Eastern Zhou** had a more difficult time maintaining control of rival states within its control. The Zhou dynasty was the period in which Chinese civilization spread to most parts of Asia. Both **Confucius** and **Lao Tzu** were active during this period. China became the preeminent state during this period.

Han Dynasty

The Han dynasty ran from approximately 206 BC to AD 220. It began when a peasant, **Liu Pang**, led a successful insurrection against the Qin dynasty leaders. The **Han** shifted the capital of China to Changan (Xian). This was the period in which **Confucianism** became the dominant political and social ideology in China. The Han developed a code of laws and a form of government based upon the proper Confucian relations between king and subject, husband and wife, and father and son. The Han dynasty saw China accrue fantastic wealth and become one of the most sophisticated and resplendent countries the world has seen. Eventually, though, peasant revolts weakened the Han and made them susceptible to overthrow.

Daoism

Next to Confucianism, **Daoism** (also Taoism) is the most important philosophy to have emerged out of China. **Taoist thought** is based on the 6th century-BC writings of **Lao Tzu**, specifically on the Tao Te Ching. Lao Tzu was a student of Confucius and taught that individuals should discover the essential nature of things and of themselves and should not seek to challenge the natural harmony of life. A proper Taoist should be patient and austere. Unlike Confucianism, Daoism contains an element of mysticism and so may be called a religion. Taoism introduced the concept of the **yin and yang**, the contrasting male and female elements that make up everything in existence and which must be harmonized in order to achieve self-realization.

Early Civilizations of Mesoamerica and South America

Mesoamerica, which is now known as Central and South America, were both host to developed civilizations 3,000 years before the arrival of Columbus. These civilizations were largely dependent upon water-supported agriculture. The most important crop in the region was **maize**. The first dominant group in this region, the **Olmecs**, was based in what is now the gulf coast of eastern Mexico. The Olmecs were known for making large and elaborate stone carvings. There were also major civilizations at this time in what is now Peru. In the Andes Mountains of that region, the **Chavin** culture developed intricate stone temples and pyramids. These sites have been explored carefully by archaeologists.

Hinduism

Hinduism is the traditional religion of India. It is expressed in an individual's philosophy and behavior, rather than in the performance of any specific rituals. **Hinduism** does not claim a founder but has evolved slowly over thousands of years; the first Hindu writings date back to the third millennium BC. There are a few concepts that are common to all permutations of Hinduism, such as the **Vedas**, which are considered to be the sacred texts of the religion. The chief aim in life for a Hindu is to be liberated from the cycle of suffering and rebirth. Hindus believe in **reincarnation** and that a person's conduct in this life will affect his or her position in the next (**karma**). Although Hinduism is frequently associated with the caste system, the two are actually unrelated.

Hindu Caste System

The Hindu caste system is a means of organizing society. It divides the populace into four groups, each associated with a part of the body of the Hindu god Purusha. The highest class is the **Brahmins**, associated with the mouth of the god. In the original system, the brahmin class was made up of priests. The second caste is the **Kshatriyas**, made up of rulers and soldiers; this caste is associated with the arms of Purusha. Next are the **Vaishyas**, associated with the legs of the god. This caste was composed of landowners, merchants, and artisans. The last group is the **Shudras**, associated with the feet of the god. This caste was composed of servants and slaves. Women do not have a place in the traditional Hindu caste system.

Judaism

Judaism was founded by **Abraham** in the 20th century BC. Abraham was called out from among the Chaldeans to enter into a covenant with God, whereby he and his descendants would receive special treatment and an inheritance of land. Abraham then moved to Canaan (near present-day Israel). Later, his descendants would move to Egypt and be enslaved. They were eventually liberated from slavery in Egypt by God through Moses, and they conquered the land of Canaan under the leadership of Joshua. Moses received from God a set of strict laws, the **Ten Commandments**; all of this is described in the **Torah**, the essential Jewish Scripture. There are also several other important books, including the Talmud, and many important commentaries by learned Jewish theologians.

Creation of Ancient Israel

Around the year 1020 BC, **Saul** became the first king of the Jewish nation, known as **Israel**. Saul's successor **David** conquered the city of Jerusalem and united all of the tribes of Israel, making Jerusalem their capital. In the 10th century BC, David's son **Solomon** built the first Jewish Temple in Jerusalem; this building was used to house the **Ark of the Covenant**, which housed the original Torah. Israel would be taken over by the **Assyrians** in the 8th century BC, and later by the **Babylonians**. Finally, in 538 BC, the Persian King Cyrus allowed the Jews to return to Jerusalem and rebuild the Temple. Israel would subsequently be taken over by the **Greeks** under Alexander, and later by the **Romans** under Pompey.

Vedic Age

The Vedic Age is the period recounted in the Indian Vedas, the earliest known records of Indian history. The dates of the **Vedic age** are considered by most to be between 2000 and 1000 BC. The oldest Vedic text is the **Rig-Veda**, which bears many Indo-Iranian elements. It is a collection of religious hymns and stories and describes a nomadic people who were ruled by a king who depended on their consent. His main duty was to protect the people. Religion in this period primarily consisted of chanting and the performing of sacrifices. During this period, elaborate rules concerning marriage were created, and the rigid social stratification that would become known as the **caste system** evolved.

Buddhism

Buddhism was created by **Gautama Siddhartha** (otherwise known as Buddha) in about 528 B.C. It was in part a response to Hinduism, which Buddha felt had become bloated with worldliness and politics. Traditional Buddhism is based upon the **Four Noble Truths**: existence is suffering, suffering is caused by desire, an end of suffering will come with Nirvana, and Nirvana will come with the practice of the **Eightfold Path**. The steps of the Eightfold Path are as follows: right views, right resolve, right speech, right action, right livelihood, right effort, right mindfulness, and right concentration. Buddhism has no deities. Buddhism did not receive any official sanction for a long time but did eventually spread and take hold in India, China, Japan, and elsewhere.

Persia

Persia is the European name for the region that is now Iran. This area has been the site of a number of vibrant cultures. The **Medes** were the first to develop there, lasting from approximately 700 to

549 BC, when they were expelled by the army of Cyrus. This great king then established the **Achaemenid dynasty**, which itself was destroyed by Alexander the Great in 330 BC. After this, a succession of peoples including the **Parthians**—rivals to Rome—inhabited the region, until a durable **Sasanian dynasty** was established in AD 224. Persia was in constant conflict with the **Byzantine Empire**, and would eventually be overtaken by the **Arabs** in the 7th century AD.

Zoroastrianism

Zoroastrianism was the state religion of Persia during the **Sasanian dynasty** between the years AD 224 and 651. It is based upon the prophecies of **Zoroaster** (also known as Zarathustra, c. 628-551 BC), a Persian who claimed to have encountered the divine being Ahura Mazda. Zoroastrians believed that the world was composed of good and evil spirits, who are in constant conflict. Fire was sacred to the Zoroastrians. Many of the concepts of Zoroastrianism would be included in Christianity, especially by the Manichean sect, who also saw the world as a struggle between absolute good and absolute evil. Zoroastrianism receded in popularity with the rise of Islam.

City-State of Athens in Ancient Greece

Ancient Greece was dominated by two city-states, **Athens** and **Sparta**. These two had very distinct cultures. Athens was a coastal city with a democratic form of government which amassed wealth by trading overseas. Athens is also known as the city that gave life to philosophy and the arts. **Socrates** engaged in his famous dialogues in the streets of Athens, and though he was eventually executed by the Athenian government for supposedly corrupting the youth, his thoughts achieved immortality in the writings of his student **Plato**. In turn, Plato's student **Aristotle** developed a strict form of reasoning that has formed the basis of much subsequent Western thought. Athens is also renowned for the architectural marvel that is the **Parthenon**.

Sparta in Ancient Greece

While Athens was known for its devotion to the arts and its democratic form of government, its rival city-state **Sparta** was devoted to agriculture and the military. Sparta was not located on the coast, and therefore the Spartans had little contact with distant peoples. Spartan society was governed by a strict class system. Most people (**helots**) worked the land of other people as virtual serfs. In the upper classes, participation in **military training** was compulsory. Indeed, Spartan youths left their families to begin military training at a young age. The Spartans did not produce any noteworthy philosophers, but as a culture, they stressed the good of the group over that of the individual. This is in stark contrast to most Athenian thought, which celebrates the achievements of the individual.

Review Video: Ancient Greece
Visit mometrix.com/academy and enter code: 800829

Greece in the Periclean and Hellenistic Ages

The **Periclean Age** in Greece, so named because Pericles was the leader of Athens during the period, took place in the 5th century BC. It was during this period that most of the great contributions to Western culture were made, including the philosophy of Socrates, the medical work of Hippocrates, and the great dramatic works of Aeschylus, Sophocles, and Euripides. The **Hellenistic Age** (4th century BC), on the other hand, is more commonly known for the military conquests made by **Alexander the Great**. If it were not for the conquests of Alexander during the Hellenistic Age, many of the innovations and achievements of the Periclean Age may not have had such a great influence on the West. It should be noted that the Hellenistic Age was not without its own great thinkers; in fact, Alexander studied as a boy under Aristotle.

Major Wars of Greece in the Periclean and Hellenistic Ages

During the **Age of Pericles**, an alliance of Greek city-states was challenged by the mighty Persians. Miraculously, the outnumbered Greeks were able to defeat the Persians at Thermopylae and Marathon, and staved off conquest. The war with the Persians impoverished the Greeks, however, and increased rivalries among the city-states. In Athens, the requirements for citizenship were loosened, though slavery remained. Conflict between Sparta and Athens culminated in the **Peloponnesian War**, won by Sparta. Eventually, the whole of Greece would be conquered by **Philip of Macedon**, who allowed the Greeks to maintain their culture and traditions. **Alexander the Great** was the son of Philip and became the master of an empire larger than any the world had ever seen. During his reign, he united many disparate peoples through a common law and exchange policy. He died at the age of 33, and his empire was divided into three parts amongst his generals.

Roman Republic

Roman civilization dates from the founding of the city in 753 BC until the defeat of the last Emperor, **Romulus Augustus**, in AD 476. The republic itself lasted from the overthrow of the monarchy in 509 BC until the empowering of the first Emperor, **Octavian Augustus**, in 27 BC. The area along the Tiber River where Rome would be built was previously inhabited by a group known as the **Etruscans**. Rome took its name from the legendary **Romulus**, who is said to have founded it after triumphing over his brother Remus. The basic structure of Roman society consisted of **patricians** at the top of the social hierarchy, who were descendants of the founders of the republic and often wealthy. Beneath the patricians were the **plebeians**, which consisted of all other freemen. Finally, at the bottom of the social hierarchy were **slaves**. Women were not included in most social or economic business, although a Roman woman's rights were often significantly preferable to her contemporaries in other civilizations. The **Roman Republic**, which was the first political arrangement of Rome, was led by two consuls who were chosen annually. The **consuls** presided over the **Senate**, made up of a permanent group of those who had been previously elected to a high-ranking magistracy (originally primarily patrician in composition), and the **Assembly**, which was solely for the plebeians. Rome had extensive laws covering individual and property rights.

Review Video: Roman Republic Part One
Visit mometrix.com/academy and enter code: 360192

Review Video: Roman Republic Part Two
Visit mometrix.com/academy and enter code: 881514

Expansion of Rome

Punic Wars

The first real challenge to the territorial expansion of Rome was the city of **Carthage**, located across the Mediterranean in North Africa. Carthage was founded by the Phoenicians. There were three major conflicts, known as the **Punic Wars**, fought between Rome and Carthage. Rome won the **First Punic War** and acquired Sicily in the process. The Carthaginian effort in the **Second Punic War** was led by Hannibal and included his famous crossing of the Alps. Hannibal was quite successful in Italy, but a combination of a war of attrition throughout Italy and the counterattacks on Carthaginian holdings in Spain and the city of Carthage itself by the Romans forced Hannibal to retreat to North Africa to defend Carthage. In the **Third Punic War**, Rome finally destroyed Carthage; in fact, it is often rumored that the victorious Romans burned Carthage to the ground and then salted the fields of their vanquished foe, a tribute to the Senator Cato the Elder's repeated cry at the end of various speeches of "*Ceterum censeo Carthaginem esse delendam*" ("Moreover, I have determined that Carthage must be destroyed").

Review Video: The Punic Wars
Visit mometrix.com/academy and enter code: 879745

Greece, Gaul, and Spain

After defeating Carthage once and for all, Rome met little resistance as it continued to acquire more territory. This was partly due to the superiority of Roman weaponry, and in part because the Romans were good at bringing conquered peoples into the fold. Rome typically allowed conquered people to maintain their native cultures, so long as they paid tribute to Rome. Rome defeated the Macedonians and took **Greece**, then conquered large portions of **Gaul** (France) and **Spain**. The vastness of the Roman Empire necessitated some advances in infrastructure technology. Romans are justly famous for their solid and durable **roads** and **aqueducts** (systems for delivering water), many of which survive today.

Grand Alliance of Julius Caesar in Rome

As Rome continued to expand, class conflicts developed between the nobility and the poor. In this era of unrest, it became possible for individual leaders to claim more power than the law had allowed previously. In 60 B.C., the famous general Julius Caesar formed the three-person alliance known as the First Triumvirate to govern Rome. The other two members were **Gnaeus Pompey Magnus** and **Marcus Licinius Crassus**. During this period, Caesar led a successful campaign against the Gauls (a people in modern-day France) and made himself richer than the entire Roman State on the proceeds from his conquest. After Crassus was killed in battle, Caesar pushed Pompey out and assumed total control of Rome, crowning himself dictator-for-life. Though Caesar was very popular with the mob, his decision to claim lifelong power alienated him from the nobility in the Senate. He was assassinated by a group of senators, led by **Marcus Iunius Brutus**, in 44 B.C.

Second Roman Triumvirate

After the assassination of Caesar in 44 B.C., Rome was mired in chaos. Those who had conspired to kill Caesar had hoped to return to the republican form of government, but instead another trio of leaders came to the fore, this time as a governmental commission of "three men for reconstituting the Republic," known as the **Triumvirate**. The Triumvirate was composed of **Marc Antony**, one of Caesar's greatest generals and a Consul at the time; **Octavius**, the nephew and testamentary heir of Caesar; and **Marcus Aemilius Lepidus**, a third wheel who was quickly made a non-entity. While Octavius stayed in Rome, Antony left for Egypt, where he stayed for a time as the guest and lover of **Cleopatra**. Eventually, infighting between Octavius and Antony led the former to mount a campaign against Egypt. When they realized that they were defeated, Antony and Cleopatra committed suicide to avoid the shame of being paraded in Octavian's triumph. Lepidus having been marginalized, Octavius (now known as Augustus) became the first **Emperor**.

Pax Romana

After the ascension of Augustus, Rome entered a period of relative tranquility. Augustus dubbed this era, which lasted about forty years, the **Pax Romana**. Rome remained an empire, although the conquered peoples were able to obtain Roman citizenship without having to forfeit their native customs. It was at this period that Rome reached its greatest geographic proportions, stretching all the way up to present-day Scotland. This was also the greatest period for **Roman artistic achievement**; both Virgil and Ovid were active during the Pax Romana, and, indeed, the Aeneid of Virgil was written in part to glorify Augustus. It was at this time that the polytheist religion of Rome was challenged first by the **Judaism** of the conquered Hebrews, and later by the early **Christians**.

Constantine and the Christians

The Roman Emperor **Constantine**, in response to the inconvenient vastness of his dominion, established an eastern capital: **Constantinople**, in AD 330. Having received a sign in the heavens which promised him victory over his rivals for the office of Emperor should he convert to Christianity, Constantine famously issued the **Edict of Milan**, in which he called for the end of the persecution of Christians, after a sound victory as promised. After this act, Christianity flourished in the Roman Empire and became the official religion of the state. A movement called **monasticism** developed within the religion, advocating the renunciation of worldly goods in favor of contemplation and prayer. After the death of Constantine, the empire once again proved unwieldy for one man, and therefore it split as it had previously, with the western half being governed from Rome and the eastern half from Constantinople. This arrangement would prove untenable, however; a Germanic tribe of **barbarians** eventually sacked Rome, and the western Roman capital fell in AD 476.

Byzantine Empire

The eastern half of the Roman Empire became known as the **Byzantine Empire**. After the fall of Rome, **Emperor Justinian** led successfully from Constantinople for a number of years. The Justinian era is especially remembered for the contributions to law and religious artwork, in particular the development of mosaics. In the years after the fall of Rome, the **Catholic Christian Church** gradually rose to fill the power vacuum. In what had been the Western Roman Empire, the Church acted completely independent of any political body, while even in the Byzantine Empire the Church was increasing in power. Only the influence of the Byzantine Emperor kept the Church from being the most powerful group in all of Europe.

Rise of Christianity

Early Christianity was a mass of competing doctrines, including various groups such as the Gnostics and Arians who all sought to have their view legitimized as the truth. Eventually, the **orthodox church**, through an ecumenical council of bishops, created in the 4th century AD the canon of New Testament texts which exists today. The apostles had created a hierarchy of bishops, priests, and deacons who stressed obedience to duly constituted church authority. By the middle of the 2nd century, Christianity began to attract intellectuals in the **Roman Empire**. Although Christians were still liable to be persecuted in the farther reaches of the empire, many turned to the Church as the empire crumbled, as the Church was all that was left of civilization, and would rebuild Europe over the next millennium.

Kingdom of Kush

Kush was a powerful African kingdom that lasted in some form from 2000 BC until AD 350. For a long time, **Kush** was based around the city of **Kerma**, in what is now Sudan. Kushites became wealthy because of their mineral resources and because of their advantageous location in the northwest corner of Africa, where they were at the crossroads of several intercontinental trade routes. There was a great deal of contact between Kush and **Egypt** in this period. In 767 BC, King Kashta of Kush defeated the Egyptians, and the Kushites had control of the entire Nile Valley. Kush would soon be weakened by the Assyrians, however, and would eventually fall prey to the **Romans**; in AD 350, the new capital of Kush, Meroe, was sacked.

Aksum (Axum)

Aksum, a town in what is now northern Ethiopia, was the capital city of one of Africa's most powerful kingdoms between the 1st and 6th centuries AD. The kings of **Aksum** were said to have descended from **Menelik**, one of the sons of the famous King Solomon. These people controlled almost all of the trade on the **Red Sea** and made a tremendous profit on the exchange of ivory. In the 4th century AD, Aksum eliminated the kingdom of **Kush** and became the predominant power in Africa. It was also during this century that Aksum was **Christianized**; it remains a hub of Ethiopian Christianity to this day. In its later stages, Aksum's control extended into southern Arabia and would eventually give way to the Persians and the Arabs.

NOK CULTURE

One of the most successful cultures of the African Iron Age was the **Nok culture**. The Nok developed **ironworking** technology before anyone else, and also created a rich artistic culture that spread throughout the West African forest region. The Nok were mainly active between the 5th and the 1st centuries BC. Their creation of iron farm implements made it possible for farmers to develop surplus crops, and thus urban centers could develop. This increase in agricultural productivity also made it possible for there to be more specialization of labor. Therefore, not only were civilizations more stable, but they were also better able to protect themselves, as they now had both better weapons made of iron and more time to train warriors.

ANCIENT GHANA

Beginning in the 7th century AD, **Ghana** was a major trading power in west Africa. It was mainly located in the areas that are now known as Mali and Mauritania. The people of Ghana grew rich by exchanging ivory and gold from the south and salt from the north. Eventually, Ghana would become an empire and would collect lavish tributes from all of the lands within its control. In the 11th century, the capital of Ghana was **Kumbi**. In 1076, however, Kumbi fell to the Almoravids, a Muslim tribe. The whole of Ghana would eventually be subsumed into the burgeoning empire of **Mali**.

ANCIENT MALI

Today, Mali is the largest nation in West Africa. Indeed, throughout African history, **Mali** has been a major power. Until the 11th century, it was a part of the empire of Ghana, a wealthy trading nation. Mali would eventually rise to prominence in its own right. The economy of Mali was based upon the rich mineral resources (especially gold) of the region. Mali reached its highest prominence during the reign of **Mansa Musa** (AD 1312-7). This ruler introduced Islam to his people, which at this time lived as far north as Morocco. The city of **Timbuktu** became a cultural center for the region, as well as a crossroads for trade routes that stretched across the Sahara. Over time, internal disputes would divide Mali into several smaller kingdoms.

SONGHAI EMPIRE

The Songhai empire flourished in West Africa between the 14th and 16th centuries. Centered in the valley of the Niger River, the **Songhai** were first organized by Christian **Berbers** in the 7th century. Four hundred years later, they established their capital at **Gao** and became an Islamic nation. Except for a brief period in which they were ruled by the empire of Mali, the Songhai controlled over a thousand miles along the Niger. Like most of the African powers, the Songhai made their money through trade. **Muhammad I**, who ruled from 1493 to 1528, expanded the empire to its greatest area. One of the weaknesses of the Songhai, however, was that they did not have a traditional means of succession, and thus frequent infighting among the powerful eventually led to the empire's demise.

THE HUNS

The Huns were a nomadic people who moved east across central Asia during the 4th century AD. The **Huns** were divided into several branches. The **White Huns** overran the Sasanian Empire and conquered many cities in the northern part of the Indian subcontinent. Another group roamed eastern Europe and established a strong empire on the Hungarian Plain around AD 400. The Huns were known for their amazing horsemanship and for being aggressive on the battlefield. It was under the guidance of **Attila** (440s) that the Huns reached their highest level of prominence. During this period, they collected tribute from many of the areas within the Roman Empire. Soon after the death of Attila, however, the Huns became complacent and lost most of their territory.

The Mongols

The Mongols, who descended from the Huns, were a nomadic group that roamed east-central Asia. Around the year AD 1206, the various **Mongol** tribes were united under **Genghis Khan**, whose empire then stretched from the Black Sea to the Pacific Ocean, and from Tibet to Siberia. After the death of Genghis, the Mongol lands were divided up. This did not, however, slow expansion; Mongols eventually controlled parts of Iran as well. **Kublai Khan** was another prominent Mongol leader; he destroyed the Song dynasty in China and replaced it with the Yuan. By the 14th century, the Mongol Empire was beginning to disintegrate. Like many of its kind, it proved too large to govern. The Ming and subsequently the Qing dynasties put the remaining Mongols under Chinese control.

Emergence of Russia

In the Middle Ages, Russia had a complicated and inefficient system of succession, which meant that the various lands were constantly being fought over, and authority was often dubious. For a long time, **Russia** was dominated by the **Mongols** (Tatars), who kept the local governments weak in order to continue receiving tributes. Moscow was able to parlay loyalty to the Tatars and colonization of other feudal estates into a great deal of power during this period. Supported by their Tatar overlords, the **Muscovite princes** were able to partition off their new lands in such a way that it became very difficult for nobles to consolidate their landholdings, which prevented any wealthy lords from ever challenging the princes of Moscow.

Steppe Peoples and Seljuk Turks

Between the years AD 1000 and 1450, invaders from the **steppes** conquered parts of Asia, the Middle East, and Europe. These people had originally been nomads, but in this period, they began to settle and become tradesmen. The clans that made up this group were loosely based on family ties; once they became stationary, they began to appoint powerful chiefs for leadership support. Near AD 1000, the **Seljuk Turks** moved from Central Asia into the Middle East. This group then controlled the trade routes between Asia, Africa, and Europe, and charged tolls on these routes, building an empire with their wealth. In 1071, the Seljuk Turks defeated the Byzantines at the **Battle of Manzikert**; a Christian defeat which would be part of the motivation for the **First Crusade**. The Seljuk Turks were known as excellent fighters and mediocre rulers; local leaders frequently ignored the central government and fought one another for control of land. This infighting weakened the group until they became prey to new nomadic invaders from Central Asia.

Poland and Hungary in Eastern Europe During the Middle Ages

During the Middle Ages, a number of different leaders tried to unite the various lands of **Poland**. These attempts were always defeated by the nobility, who preferred the country to be an oligarchy rather than a monarchy. Poland was also much involved during this period in a battle with the **Teutonic knights** over the Baltic coastline. **Hungary** was a feudal state by the beginning of the 14th century, and the various patches of land which constituted the country were ruled as if they were independent. Bishops in the **Eastern Orthodox Church** were among the largest landholders. Ostensibly, the nobility was in charge of the defense of the Hungarian people, though they rarely supplied the money and material for war.

Origins and Expansion of Islam

The religion of Islam was founded by the prophet **Muhammad** in AD 610. **Islam** is a monotheistic religion based on the **Koran**, a book of scripture according to the Muslim god, **Allah**. The practice of Islam is based on "**Five Pillars**": faith in Allah, a pilgrimage to the city of Mecca, a yearly fast during the month of Ramadan, the giving of alms, and prayer five times a day. Muhammad also asserted that Islam should be spread throughout the world. Indeed, as the Christian Church was becoming the dominant factor in Europe, Islam was spreading throughout North Africa, the Middle East, parts of Asia, and even Spain. The simultaneous ascensions of Christianity and Islam inevitably led to conflict, most notably in the **Crusades**.

Review Video: Islam
Visit mometrix.com/academy and enter code: 359164

Islamic Civilization

After the formation of Islam in the 7th century AD, it took 3 or 4 centuries to develop the institutional structures of the religion. **Islamic law** was created, and a new class of Muslim religious leaders and scholars emerged who took a prominent place in society. The Islamic civilization drew elements from its surroundings, namely the culture of the Greeks, Iranians, Christians, Jews, and Zoroastrians. At first, the Islamic Empire was ruled by a single **caliph** and a small Arab elite. As the empire expanded, however, this became untenable, and the lands were divided into a number of independent political entities. Also, factions began to emerge among Muslims, most notably between the **Sunnis** and **Shiites**, who rivaled over the true successor to Muhammad, among other issues. Because the entire Islamic world operated with a common system of trade, it quickly became very wealthy.

Review Video: The Islamic Empire
Visit mometrix.com/academy and enter code: 511181

Feudalism in Western Europe

Feudalism was the system of social and economic organization that developed in Europe in the Middle Ages (roughly AD 750 to 1300). **Feudalism** is characterized by rigid hierarchies among the various classes. At the top of the hierarchy was the **king**, and below him **lords**, who oversaw a smaller area of land. Below the lords were **noblemen** who had been granted control over farmland in exchange for their pledge of allegiance to the king. These noblemen were known as **vassals** and **subvassals**. The land managed by each vassal was known as a **fief**, and the home of the vassal was known as the **manor**. Each manor and the community surrounding it comprised a self-sufficient unit. The laws of **primogeniture** were enforced at this time, meaning that the ownership of the fief would descend to the firstborn son of the lord. Finally, the land was cultivated either by **peasants** or **serfs**; peasants were free farmers, while serfs were basically slaves who were forced to work for the lord and were bound to their lands.

Charlemagne

The emergence of the feudal system in Western Europe meant that instead of a centralized power, there were many local authorities. **Charlemagne** (AD 742-814) was a Germanic leader who tried to unify the former Western Roman Empire. In AD 800, **Pope St. Leo III** crowned Charlemagne Emperor of Rome during Christmas Mass at St. Peter's Basilica in Rome, establishing a political relationship with the **Church** that would last throughout the Middle Ages. Charlemagne allocated a great deal of power to regional leaders and did not tax his subjects. For this reason, he was unable to make many internal improvements during his reign. Nevertheless, Charlemagne is credited with promoting the arts, especially within the thriving monasteries, without which much of antiquity would not have been transcribed and thus preserved. After the death of Charlemagne, his lands were divided up among his three grandsons according to the **Treaty of Verdun**.

Holy Roman Empire

The Holy Roman Empire was the name given to the holdings of **Otto the Great** in 962, who had unified the central area of Charlemagne's empire. As in Charlemagne's day, this was a disparate group of territories, and proved difficult to govern. Otto incorporated the **Church** into his government, though he continually sought to minimize its power. One of the legacies of Otto's reign would be the rivalry between the Church and state. Gradually, the Church leaders acquired power, until they were exercising great control over the day-to-day activities of most citizens. Perhaps inevitably, this great power began to corrupt many of the Church's leaders. Indicative of the state of the Church was the often unpunished offense of **simony**, in which prestigious and important offices were bought and sold.

Review Video: The Middle Ages: The Holy Roman Empire
Visit mometrix.com/academy and enter code: 137655

Western Europe in the 12th and 13th Centuries

In the 12th century AD, the various **fiefs** in Western Europe increasingly came into contact with one another. As advances in transportation technology made trade with distant neighbors possible, there developed more necessity for specialization. Rather than be entirely self-sufficient, lords found it was more economically advantageous to perfect the cultivation of one crop and exchange that for everything else. As **trade** became more important, so did the merchants in towns, known as burghers, who wielded considerable political power. Trade arrangements led to alliances between various towns, and the whole of Western Europe became more homogenous. The distinction between **classes** also became much less pronounced during this period. There were drawbacks, however: the increasing number of people in towns, as well as the more frequent travel between towns, contributed, no doubt, to the **bubonic plague epidemic** of the mid-14th century.

Faith and Learning in Western Europe During the Late Middle Ages

Surprising though it may seem, one of the best things that happened to Christian thought during the Middle Ages was its contact with **Islam**. The complex philosophies of Muslim scholars helped spur the evolution of **Christian theology**. These, in addition to the rediscovery of ancient philosophers such as Aristotle, led Christians to begin to glorify **reason** as the God-given tool for investigating religious faith. Many assertions made by the new rational theologians, however, were dubbed **heresy** by many Church leaders, as more and more Christian thinkers were bemoaning the materialistic ways of the Church leaders. One of the leading Christian thinkers of the Middle Ages was **St. Thomas Aquinas**, whose *Summa Theologica* outlined rational explanations for the belief in God and in the miracles of Christianity.

Formation of Universities in the Middle Ages

The rapid evolution in Christian thought that took place during the Middle Ages gave rise to the formation of the first **universities**. For the first time in Western Europe, young men would move to large cities to study theology, law, and medicine at formal institutions. In addition to this trend, the academic method known as **scholasticism** was developed, in which scholars would use logic and deductive reasoning in order to analyze a work or determine something of an abstract nature. Among the so-called scholastics, two schools of thought developed: those scholars who adhered to the ideas of Plato were known as **realists**, and those who followed Aristotle were known as **nominalists**. The word *realist* is somewhat confusing when used to refer to the work of Plato, who believed that our perceptions of objects were merely perceptions of the barest shadows of their reality. Another development of Christianity in this period was **mysticism**; Christian mystics believed that they could achieve union with God through self-denial, contemplative prayer, and alms-giving.

Germany, Italy, and France in the 13th Century

During the 13th century, France was transformed from a group of disparate fiefs into a centralized monarchy by **Philip Augustus** (Philip II). His heir, Philip IV, would establish the **Estates General**, a governing body composed of representatives from each province. The Estates General contained noblemen as well as wealthy commoners. Meanwhile, Germany endured an **interregnum**, or period between kings, after the ruler died without a clear successor. Italy, as well, spent this period as a collection of strong and independent townships. In a decentralized state, it became easier for wealthy merchants to wield power. In Germany, the **Hanseatic League**, an association of merchants, set regional trade policy.

Magna Carta

England, unlike many of the other regions of Western Europe, had been accustomed to a strong monarchy. This tradition was challenged in AD 1215, when noblemen forced King John to sign the **Magna Carta**, a document which gave feudal rights back to the nobles and extended the rule of law to the middle-class burghers. The Magna Carta made the formation of the **Houses of Parliament** possible. Over time, Parliament would evolve into a two-house structure: the **House of Lords**, which contained nobles and clergy, and the **House of Commons,** which contained knights and burghers. The House of Lords was mainly occupied with legal questions, while the House of Commons dealt mainly in economic issues.

Feudalism End in Western Europe

In the late 13th century, increased contact between regions and greater representation in government culminated in a number of **peasant revolts** and **serf uprisings**. During this period, members of the clergy became even more secular and open in their greed for fame and power. This alienated many common citizens from the Church. The invention of **gunpowder** also changed the social arrangements in Western Europe; fewer noblemen were willing to participate in combat, and so the code of chivalry gave way to **mercenary soldiers**. Noblemen largely turned their attention to acquiring some of the fantastic wealth available in trade. The quality that men strived for in these days was called **virtue**, meaning a solemn dedication to the arts and sciences.

Papal Bull "Unam Sanctam" and the Crisis in the Western Church

Around the year 1300, the power of the Pope in political affairs was weakening because of the rise of strong monarchs and a spirit of nationalism. **Pope Boniface VIII** attempted to force kings to obey him but was unsuccessful. In response, Boniface issued a papal bull in 1296 that instructed **King Philip IV** of France to not tax the church; Philip ignored this command. Boniface would not relent, and issued the bull "**Unam Sanctam**," in which he declared that there are two powers on the earth, the temporal and the spiritual, with the latter always superior, and that there is no salvation outside of loyalty to the Roman Pontiff. Once again, Philip refused the claims of the Pope and decided to silence him by having him kidnapped and brought to France. Boniface was able to escape captivity but died soon afterward. This significantly weakened the political authority of the papacy.

Babylon Captivity and Schism and the Crisis in the Western Church

After the death of Pope Boniface VIII, King Philip IV of France persuaded the College of Cardinals to select a French archbishop as the next pope. This pope, **Clement V**, moved the papacy to Avignon, France, where it would remain for 67 years. Debate raged during this period as to whether a pope could be legitimate in any city other than Rome. Also, Clement's court became notorious for its extravagance. In 1378, a new pope was chosen; an Italian, who chose the name **Urban VI** to indicate that he planned on keeping the papacy in Rome. Upset with Urban's policy, 13 French cardinals selected a new pope, the French-speaking **Clement VII**. Now, there were two popes, and each one declared the other illegitimate. This confusion lasted from 1378 until 1417, with the Pope in Rome and an antipope in Avignon.

Hundred Years' War

England made a claim on the French throne in 1337, and the result was a **war** (or series of wars) that lasted for 116 years. France was angry, in return, that England had not upheld its feudal obligations to the French throne, to whom the English king was technically a distant vassal. France had the support of the Pope, but England used the innovation of the longbow to score some significant victories. It was during this war that the charismatic figure **Joan of Arc** emerged. Joan was a French peasant who led troops to several unlikely victories after being visited by God. Her deeds rallied the spirits of the French, and France eventually won. The catastrophic losses suffered by both sides had major consequences: England withdrew from contention as a land power, electing instead to develop a **navy**; in France, **Louis IX**—St. Louis—took advantage of the chaos to consolidate power in the monarchy.

Effects of the Black Death and Johannes Gutenberg

Toward the end of the Middle Ages, two events greatly shaped future events. The **bubonic plague**, also known as the Black Death, killed between 30% and 60% of the European population. The influx of people to squalid cities made the rapid spread of this disease possible. The seemingly random devastation caused by the disease caused many people to question their faith, and the power of the Church suffered as a result. The other monumental event was the invention of the **printing press** by Johannes Gutenberg in about 1436. This invention was used first to produce a cheap copy of the Bible. Soon, though, printing presses with movable type were being used to print all sorts of things, and the literacy rate in Europe rose dramatically. It immediately became possible to disseminate ideas quickly.

Review Video: An Overview of the Black Death
Visit mometrix.com/academy and enter code: 431857

Feudalism in Japan

Feudalism developed in Japan after wars in the 11th century left much of the land in the control of military leaders. These men did not actually own the land, but a complex set of rights were given to them, whereby they had the exclusive right to cultivate and profit from the land. Many Japanese were disenchanted with the central government at this time, so the idea of powerful regional leaders appealed to them. A code of ethics specific to feudalism emerged, and Japanese peasants were required to pledge loyalty to a particular lord rather than to a political ideal. One particular feudal administration, the **Minamoto**, acquired almost the entirety of Japan and replaced the central government for most people.

Mayas

The Mayas were based in Mexico's Yucatan Peninsula, Tabasco, and Chiapas, as well as in what is now Guatemala and Honduras. Between the years AD 200 and 950, they developed a sophisticated civilization, with complex religions, architecture, arts, engineering, and astronomy. The **Mayas** did have a form of hieroglyphic writing, but most of their history and folklore was preserved orally. The Mayas are responsible for creating an extremely accurate **calendar** and for first conceiving the number **zero**. The Maya civilization was supported by agriculture, but it was run by a class of priests and warriors. In the 9th century, the Mayas were overrun by Toltecs from the north, who created the legend of the feathered serpent **Quetzalcoatl**.

Maya Religion

The Mayas conceived of the universe as a flat, square earth, whose four corners and center were dominated by a god. Above the sky, there were 13 levels, and below were 9 underworlds, each dominated by a god. The sun and moon, deities in their own right, passed through all of these levels every day. Each male god had a female goddess counterpart. The Mayas also had patron gods and goddesses for various occupations and classes. Maya rulers had religious powers. Religious rituals often entailed human sacrifice and self-mutilation. The Mayas also played a ritual ball game that had religious importance; the losers of this game stood to lose their lives. Mayas developed their cities as tributes to the gods.

Aztecs

When the **Toltec empire** had been eradicated around the year 1150, the power in Mesoamerica shifted to the valley of Mexico, around three lakes. By about 1325, the **Aztecs** had seized control of this area. The Aztec civilization was organized into **city-states**, much like early medieval Europe; political intrigue and state marriages were as common among the Aztecs as among the French. The Aztecs were known as fierce warriors and were hated by their neighbors because of their brutality. According to legend, the Aztecs settled in **Tenochtitlan** after a scout saw an eagle with a serpent in its beak perched on a cactus there. The Aztecs formed alliances based on threats and forced tributes.

Incas

The Incas inhabited a huge area, from present-day Ecuador to central Chile to the eastern side of the Andes Mountains. The **Incas'** territory expanded especially after the 14th century AD. The Incas were engaged in frequent conflicts with rival groups, and they frequently enslaved the groups that they defeated. They eventually formed a permanent underclass of **serfs** in order to ensure that the lands of the military leaders would be cultivated. Incas typically dispersed rival groups in order to prevent being attacked. The Incan religion contained a god in heaven, a cult of ancestors, and a number of sacred objects and places. The Incas called themselves the **children of the Sun**.

Tang Dynasty

The Tang dynasty was in control of China from AD 618 to 907. One of the main projects pursued by the **Tang** rulers was the **unification** of the far-flung and diverse Chinese states. The early portion of the Tang dynasty is considered one of the high points in Chinese history; the economy and the arts both flourished. Under the leadership of Tang generals, Chinese soldiers would claim parts of Afghanistan, Tibet, and Korea. The Tang were also somewhat unique as Chinese leaders in that they encouraged the introduction of foreign ideas into Chinese culture. **Printing** was invented in China during this period, and thus ideas could be disseminated much more easily. The end of the Tang dynasty came after a period of internal governmental conflict.

Song Dynasty

The Song dynasty of China lasted between the years AD 960 and 1279. The **Song** rulers are credited with reuniting many portions of China that had become disjointed. Historians usually distinguish between the Northern and the Southern Song. The leaders of the Song dynasty made a deliberate effort to reduce the emphasis on military conquest; instead, they focused on developing China's **civil service**. The Song dynasty saw a rejuvenation of **Confucian philosophy** in China, as well as a renewed interest in the **arts**. Some people compare the Song dynasty with the European

Renaissance. The Song was the only dynasty in China not to be ended by internal conflict; the Song were ousted by a rebel leader instead.

Mauryan Empire

The Mauryan Empire lasted approximately between the years 321 and 185 BC. in India. It was established by the powerful leader **Chandragupta Maurya** and featured a strong military and an efficient bureaucracy. The **Mauryan empire** eventually spread as far west of the Indus River as present-day Afghanistan. At its greatest expansion, the Mauryan empire comprised almost the entirety of what is now India. The leader **Ashoka** (c. 272-232 BC) converted to Buddhism, and his rule was prosperous for rich and poor alike. After the death of Ashoka, however, the Mauryan Empire splintered, as the southern lands sought autonomy and the northern lands were subject to constant foreign invasions.

Chapter Quiz

Ready to see how well you retained what you just read? Scan the QR code to go directly to the chapter quiz interface for this study guide. If you're using a computer, simply visit the online resources page at **mometrix.com/resources719/abcteworldhist** and click the Chapter Quizzes link.

World History 1400 to 1914

Beginning of the Renaissance

In the 14th century, the turmoil caused by war and plague weakened the power of Christian theology. In its place came the philosophy of **humanism**, in which the emphasis is placed on individual potential and determination while detracting from one's attention to the realm of the divine. Humanist thought contributed to a resurgence in the arts and sciences, which eventually came to be known as the **Renaissance**. In the 14th and 15th centuries, the center of this resurgence was in **Northern Italy**, in large part because this was the crossroads of several important trade routes. Specifically, the city-states of Milan, Florence, and Venice cultivated excellent artists. Talented youths typically studied in these cities with their expenses paid by a wealthy patron; the most famous patrons were the **Medici** family in Florence.

Review Video: The Renaissance
Visit mometrix.com/academy and enter code: 123100

Italian Artists of the Renaissance

The early part of the Renaissance was dominated by the artists congregated in Northern Italy. Among them were several immortal talents. **Donatello** (1386-1466) sculpted a marvelous statue of David and was the first artist in this period to depict the naked human body (religious concerns had kept recent artists from doing so). **Botticelli** (1444-1510) is the painter of the famous Birth of Venus. **Leonardo da Vinci** (1452-1519) excelled in a number of different fields, but he is perhaps best known for painting the Mona Lisa and the Last Supper. **Michelangelo** (1475-1563), though, was probably the most famous painter and sculptor of the time; he painted the ceiling in the Sistine Chapel and sculpted the most famous statue of David.

Literature and Science in the Renaissance

Although the Renaissance is typically associated with achievements in visual art, the period also saw a magnificent outpouring of literary and scientific talent. One of the most significant works to emerge from this period was *The Prince*, by the Florentine **Niccolo Macchiavelli**. This book outlined a practical plan for political management, one that would be emulated by ruthless leaders in the future. Some of the other noteworthy authors were **Erasmus** (*In Praise of Folly*), **Sir Thomas More** (*Utopia*), **Montaigne**, **Cervantes** (*Don Quixote*), **Ben Johnson**, **Christopher Marlowe**, and, of course, **William Shakespeare**. At the same time, remarkable advances were being made in the sciences. **Copernicus** incited controversy by suggesting that the Earth revolved around the Sun; **Kepler** and **Galileo** would acquire hard data to support this claim.

Age of Exploration

The Age of Exploration is also called the **Age of Discovery**. It is generally considered to have begun in the early 15th century and continued into the 17th century. Major developments of the Age of Exploration included **technological advances** in navigation, mapmaking, and shipbuilding. These advances led to expanded European exploration of the rest of the world. **Explorers** set out from several European countries, including Portugal, Spain, France, and England, seeking new routes to Asia. These efforts led to the discovery of new lands, as well as **colonization** in India, Asia, Africa, and North America.

Review Video: Age of Exploration
Visit mometrix.com/academy and enter code: 612972

Role of Economics in the Age of Exploration

At the same time that the Renaissance was reinvigorating European cultural life, a desire to explore the world abroad was growing. Indeed, the ability to make long voyages was facilitated by the advances in **navigational technology** made around this time. The main reason for exploration, though, was **economic**. Europeans had first been introduced to eastern goods during the Crusades, and the exploits of Marco Polo in the 13th century had further whetted the western appetite for contact with distant lands. This increasing focus on exploration and trade caused a general shift in the balance of power in Europe. Landlocked countries, like Germany, found that they were excluded from participating in the lucrative new economy. On the other hand, those countries which bordered the **Atlantic** (England, France, Spain, and Portugal) were the most powerful players.

Obstacles to Exploration by Europe Before 1400

Before 1400, few Europeans knew anything about the world. When **Christopher Columbus** read of the exploits of the Italian Marco Polo, however, he was inspired to seek out new trade routes. Also, **Prince Henry** of Portugal established a navigation institute that encouraged sailors to explore. For a long time, extended sea voyages were restricted by a lack of navigational and seafaring technology; the inventions of the compass, astrolabe, and caravel remedied this situation. There was also a high cost associated with long travels (around 1400); however, new monarchs in France, England, Spain, and Portugal decided that they were willing to pay a high price to get a piece of the spice trade. Finally, the question of a motive for exploration was answered by the increasing fervor for missionary work, as well as the economic necessity of developing new trade routes.

Major European Explorers

Vasco da Gama was the first European to sail around the Cape of Good Hope, on the southern tip of what is now South Africa. This made it possible to reach Asia by boat. **Balboa** explored Central America and was the first European to view the Pacific Ocean. **Magellan** is remembered as the first to circumnavigate the globe. **Cortes** was a powerful commander who subjugated the Aztecs in what is now Mexico; he used great brutality to achieve his ends. **Pizarro**, like Cortes, was a conquistador; he conquered the Incas in what is now Peru. **Amerigo Vespucci**, from whose name the word *America* was derived, mapped the Atlantic coast of South America and was able to convince stubborn Europeans that these lands were not a part of India.

Joint-Stock Companies at the Time of the Age of Exploration

As exploration created new opportunities for amassing wealth, **Portugal** enjoyed special favor because of its excellent location and cordial relations with many of the Muslim nations of North Africa. The ruler of Portugal at this time was even known as Prince Henry "the Navigator" (1394-1460). In order to solidify trade arrangements, European rulers began to think about colonizing foreign lands. In order to fund these expensive trips, a new kind of business known as the **joint-stock company** was developed. In a joint-stock company, a group of merchants would combine their resources to pay for the passage of a vessel. These groups would later be influential in securing colonial charters for many of their agents. One of the most powerful examples was the **Muscovy Company of England**, which controlled almost all trade with Russia.

Mercantilism at the Time of the Age of Exploration

As foreign trade became the most important part of every nation's economy, the economic theory of **mercantilism** became popular. According to mercantilism, a nation should never import more than it exports. Of course, it is impossible for every country to achieve this goal at the same time, so European countries were in fierce competition at all times. The solution that most nations pursued was to establish **colonies**, because these could supply resources for export by the mother country without really being considered imports. This rush to colonize had disastrous consequences for the indigenous peoples of the Americas and Africa. Europeans often looted the Native Americans for anything of value, and their need for cheap labor to cultivate the land there spawned the **African slave trade**.

Reformation

A response to corruption in the Catholic Church and lapses in enforcement of the basic tenets of the faith, such as those against simony, the **Reformation** was a movement that called for a return to what many believed to be a simpler message of salvation that they felt to be more scripturally accurate. Many people in this time were outraged by the vast landholdings and stuffed coffers of the Church, which they felt should be concerned with tending to the spiritual health of its members. In 1440, the invention of the **printing press** had made it possible for ideas to be disseminated more widely, and authors of the Renaissance had sharply criticized the greed of the clergy. People were also angered by the selling of **ecclesial offices** and especially the selling of **indulgences**, in which a person would pay money to have one's time in purgatory shortened. Selling salvation was indeed against the tenets of the Church, but was often largely unenforced. The general distrust of the Church in this period is known as **anticlericalism**.

Martin Luther

Martin Luther was a German friar who first became famous for criticizing the Catholic Church's sale of indulgences. In **1517**, in accordance with the tradition of theological debate, **Luther** posted his critique of this practice on the door of his local church; the document known as the "**Ninety-five Theses**" won him immediate fame. Luther then set about undermining the institution of the Church, arguing that individuals did not need the help of clergy to establish a strong relationship with God. Luther went even further, stating that faith, rather than obedience to arbitrary Church rules, would be what got individuals into heaven. The final straw for the Church came when Luther directly challenged the Pope, declaring that no one man could be the perfect interpreter of Scripture. Luther was excommunicated but continued to spread his message. Germany was then wracked by a war between the Lutherans of the north and the Catholics of the south. The **Peace of Augsburg** in 1555 was the resolution to this conflict, in which the subjects of a prince would follow that prince's faith, a practice referred to as *cuius regio, cuius religio*—literally, "whose jurisdiction, whose religion."

Review Video: Martin Luther and the Reformation
Visit mometrix.com/academy and enter code: 691828

Protestants

Inspired by Luther, many other critics of Catholic excess joined together throughout Europe. These groups were known collectively as **Protestants**. One of the largest sects of Protestants was the **Calvinists**, named after founder John Calvin. This group believed in the idea of predestination, or that God had already fixed each person's eternal destiny, and that only the Elect would join Him in heaven. Naturally, most people believed themselves to be among the Elect. In England, **King Henry VIII** split from the Catholic Church after his request for an annulment from Catherine of Aragon was denied by the Pope. Henry established the **Church of England** with himself as leader, and had five more wives before his death.

Review Video: The Protestants
Visit mometrix.com/academy and enter code: 583582

Counter-Reformation

After being bombarded by Protestant attacks for years, the **Catholic Church** finally began to make some positive changes. This program was known as the **Counter-Reformation**, and it was aimed at stopping the spread of Protestantism. For instance, the sale of indulgences was halted, and more authority was given to local bishops. The Church reaffirmed many of its core teachings (such as the earning of indulgences, transubstantiation, veneration of the Virgin Mary, the necessity of works, etc.) yet admitted its errors with regard to simony and abuses of clerical power, which were quickly remedied. One of the most influential men of this movement was **Sir Ignatius Loyola**, a Spaniard who founded the **Society of Jesus (the Jesuits)** to promote the Catholic interpretation of Scripture. The **Council of Trent** was a 20-year meeting that determined the official Catholic interpretation on all matters of theology. The Counter-Reformation also saw the re-emergence of the **Inquisition**, in which heretics were sought out and punished.

Review Video: The Counter-Reformation
Visit mometrix.com/academy and enter code: 950498

Introduction of the Era of European Monarchies (1500-1650)

Between the years 1500 and 1650, most of the major European powers were led by **absolute monarchs**, who claimed a divine right to rule. These European monarchies often consolidated their power by marrying into one another. The strength of the monarchies fostered a resurgent spirit of **nationalism** and consequently led to more frequent conflicts between nations. In 1500, **Spain** was probably the most powerful nation in Europe, because of her lucrative colonies and impressive Armada. Over the next century and a half, however, **France** and **England** would emerge as the dominant powers in the region. **Germany** and **Russia**, though largely excluded from shipping, were still powerful during this period.

Review Video: Absolute Monarchs: An Overview
Visit mometrix.com/academy and enter code: 678546

Review Video: Absolute Monarchs: France
Visit mometrix.com/academy and enter code: 953883

Review Video: Absolute Monarchs: Germany
Visit mometrix.com/academy and enter code: 562601

Review Video: Absolute Monarchs: Russia
Visit mometrix.com/academy and enter code: 974242

Review Video: Spanish Government in the 1500s
Visit mometrix.com/academy and enter code: 735727

Powers of Spain Between 1500 and 1650

The height of Spanish power began with the reign of **King Ferdinand** and **Queen Isabella**; these monarchs promoted exploration and became fantastically rich as a result. The Hapsburg **King Charles V** would increase Spain's prominence and territory, because he had acquired lands in France, Austria, and Germany through inheritance. Spain was drawn into a number of conflicts over these new possessions, however: France disputed his claim to parts of Italy, and the Ottoman Turks challenged his Armada in the Mediterranean. Charles V would finally be forced to abdicate the throne, leaving his brother **Ferdinand I** in control of Austria and Germany, and his son **Philip II** in control of Spain and some western lands. During Philip's reign, most of these possessions would be lost; particularly bitter was the loss of the Netherlands, which quickly became a trading power in their own right.

Pizarro and the Incas

Francisco Pizarro (c. 1478-1541) was a Spanish explorer. He lived for a time in what is now Panama, where he heard tales of the fabulous wealth enjoyed by the **Incas** in the Andes Mountains. **Pizarro** was determined to conquer this empire, and with 168 men he reached the Incan city of Tumbes in 1532. At this time, the Incas were in the middle of a civil war. Pizarro used this to his advantage; he massacred one side and took their leader prisoner. In order to free himself, the leader arranged a huge ransom, which Pizarro collected and then ignored, killing the leader anyway. Soon, Spaniards conquered the Incan city of **Cuzco** and installed a puppet regime. After some turmoil, Pizarro took over the leadership of **Peru** until his assassination in 1541.

Cortez and his Relationship with the Aztecs

Hernán Cortez (1485-1547) was a Spanish conquistador. He assisted in the conquest of **Cuba** and lived there until 1518, when he was assigned to lead an expedition into **Mexico**. He and 700 men landed on the Mexican shore, and he promptly had his ships burnt in order to indicate his sincerity about establishing a foothold in the country. **Cortez** then led his troops into **Tenochtitlan**, the capital of the **Aztec Empire**. They were received graciously by the Aztec ruler, **Montezuma**, whom they immediately enslaved. The Aztecs tried to revolt against the Spanish influence, but Cortez formed a coalition with other anti-Aztec groups and brutally eliminated the Aztec uprising. Cortez went on to rule "New Spain" for a number of years.

Government of France Between 1500 and 1650

While England was undergoing a turbulent transition from an absolute to a limited monarchy, **France** was governed by a succession of powerful and talented Bourbon monarchs. The **Estates General**, the French counterpart to the British Parliament, was not especially powerful. During a period in which the Bourbon heir was too young to govern himself, the charismatic **Cardinal Richelieu** governed France. Cardinal Richelieu was a Catholic, of course, but he did not persecute the French protestant Huguenot sect. Rather, he compromised with his enemies in an attempt to consolidate the power of the French crown. Cardinal Richelieu also established a strong bureaucracy, known as the ***noblesse de la robe***.

Government of Germany Between 1500 and 1650

Unlike many of the other Western European powers in 1500, **Germany** was still essentially just a collection of disjointed city-states. The **Hapsburg** family was powerful there, but the lands they called their **Holy Roman Empire** were not well organized, and the Hapsburgs were weak compared to other European leaders. The **Peace of Augsburg**, which had quelled disputes between Lutherans and Catholics, was destroyed by the **Thirty Years' War** (1618-48), which began when Protestants challenged the authority of the Hapsburg emperor. Germany would become so chaotic and disjointed during this period that other nations would step in, whether to seize some land or to help out one side or the other. The brutality of this war left Germany in a state of turmoil.

Russian Rule Between 1500 and 1650

As the nations of Western Europe were beginning to rely on foreign trade almost exclusively to support themselves, **Russia** remained a feudal nation. After the Mongols were overthrown, Russia was ruled by a succession of **Czars**, and Russia was largely excluded from the cultural rejuvenation of the Renaissance period. Instead, Russians suffered through the reign of **Ivan the Terrible** (1530-84), a fierce ruler who pushed the borders out in the east with horrible brutality and suffocated any rivals or critics. Ivan's reign was so oppressive that Russia could not develop a merchant class to rival those of the Western European powers, despite having some impressive natural resources.

SCIENTIFIC REVOLUTION

The rapid advance in learning known as the **Scientific Revolution** was a product of the systematic form of inquiry known as the **scientific method**. With the scientific method, learning is incremental: a question is posed, a hypothetical solution is offered, observations are made, and the hypothesis is either supported or refuted. The consistency of the method made it easy for scientific discoveries to be transferred from one country to another. Along with a standardized form of **measurement**, the development of the scientific method gave scientists a common language. Scientists also benefited from the development of powerful **telescopes** and **microscopes**.

MAJOR FIGURES

After **Copernicus** startled the world by challenging the geocentric (that is, earth-centered) model for the universe, Italian **Galileo Galilei** supplied scientific experiments that proved the accuracy of Copernicus' theory. One of the philosophical heroes of the Scientific Revolution was Frenchman **Rene Descartes**, who attempted to base his beliefs about the world upon empirical and provable facts: most famously, "I think, therefore I am." **Francis Bacon** was an English intellectual who wrote copiously on the possibilities for science to improve the human condition. **Sir Isaac Newton** excelled in many fields but is best known for his theories of motion and gravitation. Newton helped create the general idea that objects in the world behave in regular and predictable ways.

Review Video: The Scientific Revolution
Visit mometrix.com/academy and enter code: 974600

ENGLAND DURING THE TUDOR AND STUART RULINGS

For many years, England was ruled by the **Tudor** family. **Henry VIII**, the founder of the Anglican Church, had been a Tudor, and his daughter **Elizabeth** continued his policies. During the Elizabethan age in England, trading and exploration increased, and the Spanish Armada, sent to overthrow Elizabeth as a protestant heretic, was defeated. After Elizabeth died in 1603, the **Stuart** family ascended to the throne. The Stuart period would be marked by conflict. Both **James I** and **Charles I** butted heads with Parliament over the issue of taxation, and there were also continual conflicts between **Puritans** (followers of John Calvin) and **Anglicans** (adherents of the Church of England). The Puritans joined with Parliament in opposition to the monarchy.

CROMWELL AND WILLIAM AND MARY

The alliance of Parliament and the Puritans was led by **Oliver Cromwell**. His army was successful in deposing and executing **King Charles I**, and Cromwell was subsequently installed as **Protector of England**. Cromwell's rule was undermined by Anglican nobles and clergy who disliked his Puritanism. After the death of Cromwell, England was ruled by the two sons of Charles I, **Charles II** and **James II**, the latter of which was forced to abdicate by Parliament. After this period of relative chaos, **William and Mary** of the Netherlands were asked to rule England in a limited monarchy. This shift in power was known as the **Glorious Revolution**. The **Declaration of Rights** that limited the power of the monarchy gave Parliament more power and made possible a long period of tranquility.

THE ENLIGHTENMENT

Between the years 1600 and 1770, political and social philosophy in Europe underwent a tremendous change, known collectively as the **Enlightenment**. Just as Northern Italy had been the center of the Renaissance, so now **Paris** was the hub of progressive thought. The collection of philosophers, who sought to bring every subject under the authority of reason, included both **deists** (those who believed in God) and **atheists** (those who did not). The study known as **political science** first emerged during this period. Intellectuals began to question the divine right that had been claimed by absolute monarchs in the past; they sought to determine which was the best form of government for all the citizens of the country.

Review Video: Age of Enlightenment
Visit mometrix.com/academy and enter code: 143022

Major Figures

One of the most sparkling wits of the Enlightenment period belonged to the Frenchman **Voltaire** (1694-1778). He challenged the authority of the Church, declaring that people should tolerate the views of others and that no one man or group had a monopoly on absolute truth. **Thomas Hobbes** (1598-1679) was one of the most influential political theorists of the period. In his masterpiece "Leviathan," he declared that the base impulses of the people had to be restrained by a powerful and just monarch. **John Locke** (1632-1704), on the other hand, declared that men were born with natural rights which could not be justly denied them. **Rousseau** (1712-78), a Swiss philosopher, asserted that the government only ruled so long as it did so to the satisfaction of the general will of the people.

Peace of Westphalia and Louis XIV

The monarchs of the Enlightenment period found themselves under increasing pressure to be tolerant and benevolent. In Western Europe, so-called "enlightened despots" governed in order to promote the best interests of their subjects; this was probably done more to retain power than to express any profound solidarity with the commoners. France had become the central power on the European continent after the **Peace of Westphalia** (1648), which ended the **Thirty Years' War** and weakened Germany. The long reign of **Louis XIV** of France was characterized by grandiosity and the cultivation of the arts. Louis spent considerable effort trying to acquire new territories for France and glory for himself, and so alarmed the other European powers with his swiftness from victory to victory that many former enemies allied against France.

Creation of Prussia and Contributions of Frederick the Great

The **Peace of Westphalia** (1648) established the independence of several small sections of Germany; chief among these new states was Prussia. **Frederick the Great** (1712-86) became the ruler of **Prussia** in 1740 and displayed marvelous efficiency and benevolence. He made a genuine effort to allow for the coexistence of all the religious groups in Prussia, and also worked to improve the lives of the serfs. Frederick also encouraged immigration to Prussia, which brought in new ideas and technological advances. Prussia, which had long suffered economically because of its lack of a coastline, now became a producer of luxury goods like porcelain and silk.

Russia During the Rule of Peter the Great and Catherine the Great

Peter the Great (1672-1725) was responsible for the transformation of Russia from an impoverished agricultural nation to a strong commercial nation. Peter was enamored of the ways of the western European nations and made several trips to other capitals to learn the intricacies of Enlightenment politics and trade. **St. Petersburg** was intended to be a Russian city in the style of Paris or Berlin. Peter's innovations revitalized the economy, but they also set a standard for decadence that would be carried on by future czars. **Catherine II**, otherwise known as Catherine the Great, ruled from 1762 to 1796 and implemented many Enlightenment policies in education and the arts. Nevertheless, in the remote provinces of Russia, the **feudal system** endured, and the economy remained stunted.

French Revolution

Causes

Before the revolution, France was governed by an absolute monarch and, with regard to matters of taxation, the **Estates General**, which had been formed in order to represent the common people. The Estates General was composed of three estates: the clergy (**First Estate**), nobility (**Second Estate**), and everyone else (**Third Estate**). Unfortunately, this body had been marginalized by a series of powerful monarchs, and it was arranged such that the largest group by far, the Third Estate, only had one-third of the vote. In any case, the Third Estate usually found its desires opposed by the other estates. Another source of anger for the middle class and peasants was the **tax structure**; the nobles and clergy were not forced to pay taxes, and thus the burden of France's depressed economy fell upon the Third Estate.

King Louis XVI and National Assembly

Aware of the injustice of the French tax policy, **King Louis XVI** tried to pass some reforms but was repeatedly thwarted by the greedy nobles and clergy. The **Third Estate** was infuriated and refused to vote in the Estates General anymore. Instead, prominent members of the middle class banded together to form the **National Assembly**, which purported to represent the interests of common Frenchmen. At the same time, the peasants were in full revolt. On July 14, 1789, they stormed the Parisian prison known as the **Bastille**. The success of this riot inspired more peasants to clamor for representation, and the diversion it caused kept the government from dealing with the National Assembly.

Declaration of the Rights of Man

After the storming of the Bastille and the formation of the National Assembly in 1789, the French middle and lower classes joined together and established a new government with the slogan "**Liberty, Equality, Fraternity**." This government quickly reformed the tax code and declared that government offices would henceforth be filled on the basis of merit. The National Assembly also eliminated serfdom and drafted a **Declaration of the Rights of Man**, which was similar to the American Bill of Rights. The National Assembly then seized the lands that belonged to the Church and eliminated the feudal rights of the aristocracy. Soon, there was dissension within the Third Estate, and the revolution became more radical and violent.

French Revolution and the Reign of Terror

As the government established by the Third Estate descended into chaos, the radical Jacobin leader **Robespierre** took charge. He had an idealistic vision of what France could become, and he was willing to kill thousands in order to see it realized. The **guillotine** provided a swift way to execute scores of opponents, a group that included anyone who dared challenge the Jacobin party line or was suspected of retaining their Catholic faith in the new culture of state-mandated atheism. Among those executed were **King Louis XVI** and his wife, **Marie Antoinette**. After a while, the French tired of the violence and turmoil of the **Reign of Terror**, and Robespierre himself fell victim to the guillotine. A group of five prominent men, known as the **Directory**, was established to restore calm. This group would last until 1799, when it was overthrown in a coup that would eventually bring **Napoleon Bonaparte** to power.

Rise of Napoleon Bonaparte

Napoleon Bonaparte (1769-1821) began his career as a French military commander, scoring major victories in Austria and England. Upon his return to the chaos of France, he led a coup and was installed as the leader of France. He was subsequently elected by a popular vote. Almost immediately, **Napoleon** reformed French education, agriculture, and infrastructure. The main object of Napoleon's rule, however, was the acquisition of territory both in Europe and in the New World. Napoleon's troops quickly conquered Austria, Portugal, Spain, and Prussia. Napoleon, who modeled himself after Charlemagne in many ways, then crowned himself **emperor**. The French empire proved too large to manage, however, and Napoleon further weakened himself with a disastrous campaign against Russia.

Review Video: The French Revolution: Napoleon Bonaparte
Visit mometrix.com/academy and enter code: 876330

INDEPENDENCE STRUGGLE IN LATIN AMERICA

When Spain fell to Napoleon's forces in 1809, the provinces of **Chile** and **Buenos Aires** both declared themselves independent. At this time, **Peru** was the stronghold of Spanish power in the New World, and therefore the rebels attacked the government there. Led by the Argentinean **Jose San Martin**, rebels entered Lima and declared Peru an independent state in 1821. The greatest military leader of the independence movement, however, was **Simon Bolivar**. He had traveled extensively in Europe and used his knowledge of the enemy to run the Spaniards out of Colombia, Venezuela, and Central America. Bolivar eventually seized control of Peru and hoped to form a great union of South American nations, but this alliance was eventually torn asunder by internal feuds.

FALL OF NAPOLEON

After Napoleon's debacle in Russia debilitated his military, revolts sprung up in many of the nations that he had conquered, and Napoleon was overthrown. The leaders of the countries that had overthrown Napoleon met in Vienna to decide how to respond to him. These three men, **Prince von Metternich** of Austria, the English **Duke of Wellington**, and **Alexander I** of Russia, were constantly in disagreement, however, and Napoleon used this opportunity to return from his exile on the Isle of Elba in the Mediterranean and reclaim power. Finally, Napoleon was defeated at **Waterloo** and sent into permanent exile. The allies met again at the **Congress of Vienna** in 1815 where France was not treated too harshly, and it was determined that a balance of power should be maintained in Europe to ensure that no one in the future tried to dominate the continent.

OPIUM WAR

The Opium War lasted between the years 1839 and 1842. It began because the British kept trafficking **opium** from India into China because they wanted to trade with the Chinese, and opium was the only product that China could not produce for itself. The Chinese government, however, was appalled by the effect that the drug had on its citizens and mounted a serious anti-opium campaign. When British merchants appealed to their leaders, the British navy was sent in order to force the Chinese to accept the opium. The British ended up seizing several Chinese cities, including Shanghai and Nanking. The war ended with the **Treaty of Nanking** in 1842; China was forced to cede Hong Kong to the British, and several Chinese ports had to be left open for trade.

Review Video: Anti-Colonial Struggles: The Opium War
Visit mometrix.com/academy and enter code: 111806

TAIPING REBELLION

The Taiping Rebellion lasted in China between the years 1850 and 1864. It was a religious and political rebellion against the government of the **Manchus**, led by the Christian **Hung Hsiu-ch'uan**. The rebels advocated the public ownership of land and a self-sufficient economy. They wanted to rid China of the encroaching influences of foreign merchants. Hung's troops were able to conquer

Nanking and make it the capital of their "Great Peaceful Heavenly Dynasty." Internal feuds weakened the Taiping, however, and the western powers (concerned that they would lose the Chinese market) helped to oust them in 1864. The **Taiping Rebellion** was by far the bloodiest war of the 19th century.

Meiji Reform

In 1854, an American group led by **Commodore Matthew Perry** forced Japan to open its ports to foreign merchants. Japan had been closed to the West for 200 years. The Japanese people were not pleased with this development, and they blamed the **Tokugawa shogun** (the military leader of the period). In 1867, the shogun resigned and **Emperor Matsuhito** declared that he was now in charge. The Japanese capital was moved from Kyoto to Edo (which was renamed Tokyo). The ensuing period in Japanese history is known as the **Meiji Period**. During it, the feudal system was abolished, and Western ideas became popular. The samurai had their land right revoked and were eventually eliminated altogether. In the late 19th century, Japanese leaders began to turn their attentions to expansion onto the Asian continent; in the Sino-Japanese war, they conquered parts of China and Korea.

Boxer Rebellion

The Boxer Rebellion was a peasant uprising in China around the turn of the 20th century. The rebels aimed to overthrow the **Manchu government** and to cast all foreigners out of China. The rebels were known as the **Boxers** because they practiced certain mystical boxing rituals. After Japan had defeated China in 1895, the Japanese had exercised a great deal of influence on the Chinese economy. Around 1900, Boxers began to kill foreign merchants and diplomats. An international force was assembled to defeat the Boxers. During the ensuing fight, the city of **Peking** was almost entirely destroyed. Eventually, the western powers prevailed and forced the Boxer leaders to sign an incredibly unfavorable treaty.

Review Video: Anti-Colonial Struggles: The Boxer Rebellion
Visit mometrix.com/academy and enter code: 352161

Industrial Revolution

English Textile Industry

The **Industrial Revolution** in Europe in the 19th century produced immediate and far-reaching changes in the social structure. **England** was perhaps the first to feel the effects of rapid industrialization; the factory system for manufacturing textiles was implemented, meaning that individuals were only required to do one in the series of tasks required to prepare a piece of cloth. This division of labor increased productivity. New energy sources, such as the steam engine, also made fabulous increases in productivity possible. Coal was introduced as an aid to the iron-smelting process, and the mass production of cotton textiles was soon propelling the English economy.

Social Changes

With the success of the textile industry, more and more workers were needed in the European cities, and therefore people began to abandon their country lives and take factory jobs in town. This rapid **urbanization** created a new **middle class** in Europe, and it also created a number of problems. Most cities did not have the infrastructure to support such an explosion in population, and as such, disease, crime, and poverty were common. The booming success of industry made many people rich as investors and merchants, and therefore the middle class assumed even more political power in Europe. **Social mobility** was infinitely more possible in this economic environment, encouraging many people to stick with jobs that were demeaning and not especially lucrative.

Working Class and Luddites

As people flooded the cities to work in the booming factories, large landowners consolidated the farmlands they left behind. **Working-class** individuals were probably not pleased with their new lives; 18-hour days, low wages, and dangerous machinery were among the problems faced by this new underclass. Oftentimes, women and children were employed for the most menial jobs, and they were paid less than men. A small rebellion, led by a group called the **Luddites**, tried to resist the tide of industrialization and were known for vandalizing factory equipment. Still, most individuals were enticed by the prospect of upward mobility that the new, fluid class system offered, and were willing to endure hardship in exchange for hope.

Review Video: The Industrial Revolution
Visit mometrix.com/academy and enter code: 372796

Review Video: Industrialization
Visit mometrix.com/academy and enter code: 893924

Nationalism in 19th-Century Europe

In the 19th century, the spirit of nationalism that had been building in Europe since the Middle Ages reached a critical mass. **Nationalism** refers to pride in the traditions, culture, language, and past of a certain nation of people, and not necessarily to pride in one's country. This is important to note, because in the 19th century, there were many nations of people thrown together as parts of a larger kingdom. The rising tide of nationalism, then, was a concern to the ruling **monarchs**, who hoped to hold together disparate nations under their control. Russia, for instance, contained a wide variety of cultures and languages under one leadership.

Review Video: Historical Nationalism
Visit mometrix.com/academy and enter code: 510185

Classical Liberalism in 19th-Century Europe

The political and economic philosophies of the Enlightenment laid the foundation for 19th-century **classical liberalism. Adam Smith's** "The Wealth of Nations," written in 1776, introduced the concept of the "invisible hand," suggesting that market forces, if left largely to operate freely, could lead to economic prosperity. Although Smith's work preceded the Industrial Revolution, his ideas influenced later classical liberals who championed free-market policies. Another influential thinker, **Thomas Malthus**, in "An Essay on the Principle of Population" (1798), wrote that unchecked population growth would outstrip food supply, leading to famine and disease. While his work was later used to justify laissez-faire economic policies, Malthus himself advocated for population control measures rather than the outright suffering of the poor.

Social Liberalism in 19th-Century Europe

Social liberalism developed in the late 19th century as an alternative to classical liberalism. **Social liberalism** declares that political problems can be solved by the work of liberal institutions in the government. Unlike the classical liberals, social liberals believe that the government should exercise some influence on the **economy** and should extend some basic **welfare services** to the people. Social liberalism aimed to improve life for the poor and disadvantaged. Social liberals were also very outspoken on issues of civil rights and individual liberties. Some of the most famous social liberals are **Jeremy Bentham**, **John Stuart Mill**, and **John Dewey**.

Emergence of Socialism in 19th-Century Europe

Socialism is a political philosophy which declares that the economic means of production should be owned by the workers. This control may either be exercised directly by the workers through local councils or by the state with the consent of the workers. Socialists hope thereby to create a state of **social equality** and an even **distribution of wealth**. Not surprisingly, this movement was most popular among the working classes in 19th-century Europe. Socialists at this time declared that capitalism served only the interests of the very wealthy and exploited everyone else. In their view, a socialist society would provide a greater reward for hard work and would create harmonious societies. Socialism and communism come from the same ideological lineage, but they differ in some ways. Generally speaking, socialism and communism both hope to have the means of production controlled by a collective or governing organization and not owned privately. **Socialism** would allow for individuals to continue to have private property, whereas **communism** would eliminate private property and have the collective or state regulate the distribution of wealth.

Review Video: Communism vs. Socialism
Visit mometrix.com/academy and enter code: 917677

Emergence of Marxism in 19th-Century Europe

The political theories of socialism and communism both take their inspiration from the works of **Karl Marx** (1818-83). Marx declared that economics has been the primary determinant in history and that the history of society is nothing more than a "history of class struggle." Marx asserted that problems have been created in situations where the material that a worker produces is worth more than the compensation he receives for his work. The surplus goes to the capitalist owner, and the worker is caught in a situation where he can never get ahead. The inevitable result, according to Marx, is a revolution of the working class (which he called the **proletariat**) and the installation of an economic system similar to socialism or communism.

Review Video: Karl Marx
Visit mometrix.com/academy and enter code: 362061

19th-Century British Politics

During the 19th century, the memory of Napoleon and the balance of power established by the **Congress of Vienna** prevented any large conflicts. The **Industrial Revolution** had made Britain the wealthiest and most powerful nation in Europe. The rise of a rich middle class caused the British Parliament to alter voting laws so that more of the wealthy would have influence. This was done with the **Reform Act of 1832**; in 1833, Britain abolished slavery in its colonies. This was not enough for the many working-class Britons, however, and they lobbied long and hard for universal suffrage until it was finally granted in the 1880s. The British movement for universal suffrage was known as **Chartism**.

Review Video: 19th Century Politics: Britain
Visit mometrix.com/academy and enter code: 266214

19th-Century French Politics

Internal turmoil caused France to miss out on much of the wealth of the Industrial Revolution. After the demise of Napoleon, **Louis XVII** had been restored to the throne by the **Congress of Vienna**. He was succeeded by the archconservative **Charles X**, who was quite unpopular and was chased off the throne in the **July Revolution of 1830**. In his place came **Louis Philippe**, who administered over a fairly stable country for eighteen years until he was deposed in the revolution of 1848. Next came

Napoleon III. Elected the emperor of France in 1851, he remained in power until the French defeat in the **Franco-Prussian War of 1870**. From 1870 until 1940, France would be governed by a constitutional and democratic government that was, for the most part, conservative.

19th-Century German Political System

Ever since the end of Charlemagne's empire, Austria and Germany had not been unified as a single nation. This was finally achieved by the Prussian **Otto von Bismarck** after a long period of suppression of German nationalists. Bismarck's unification of **Prussia** was mainly aimed at defeating the rival Hapsburgs, who controlled Austria. When Prussia won the **Austro-Prussian** and **Franco-Prussian wars** in quick succession, Bismarck declared that he had achieved his ends and unified the German empire. He oversaw the creation of the **Reichstag**, a legislative body that would provide representation to the middle and lower classes. Germany threw itself into the project of industrialization.

19th-Century Italian Political System

Italy, like Germany, had really been more of a disjointed collection of independent city-states than a nation in its own right. In the 19th century, however, there was a drive to unify the region. A leader from the Piedmont region, **Camillo Cavour**, tried to bring the various city-states together through diplomacy rather than combat. This process took a very long time but was eventually completed in the 1870s. **Northern Italy**, which had intimate contact with Germany, became industrialized during this period, and the city of Milan enjoyed immense growth. **Southern Italy**, on the other hand, remained largely rural. This distinction between the two halves of Italy would be a source of conflict in the future.

19th-Century Russian Political System

At the beginning of the 19th century, much of Russia was still mired in an impoverished, quasi-feudal state. After the death of **Alexander** in 1825, the **Decembrists** tried to force the incoming Czar to adopt a constitution allocating some power to the people. The next czar was **Nicholas I**, who used secret police to try to eliminate the roots of the popular insurrection. This policy of suppression only further isolated Russia from the rest of Europe, which was at that time reducing the power of the monarch. Russia later lost the **Crimean War** to Britain, France, and the Ottoman Empire, and many Russians bemoaned the backward state of their country. Finally, a new czar, **Alexander II**, freed the serfs and tried to industrialize. This happened slowly.

Russian Revolution of 1905

At the turn of the 20th century, **Russia** was torn by the trends of industrialism and imperialism. The country was still being operated as an absolute monarchy, and was behind on social reforms common to the rest of Europe. Russia was trying to undergo rapid industrial expansion in the cities. Russia experienced a humiliating defeat of their navy in the **Russo-Japanese War,** causing increased labor unrest and dissatisfaction with the strong monarchy. The socialist party in Russia split into the **Bolsheviks**,who favored immediate socialist reform, and the **Mensheviks,** who favored gradual reforms and cooperation. When a peaceful demonstration against the czar was brutally suppressed, rebel forces made up of political activists, peasants, and workers became energized, leading to the **Russian Revolution of 1905.** This revolution continued with revolts by peasants and soldiers, until the czar promised to create a constitutional monarchy with a powerful legislative body, known as the **Duma**. These changes promised civil liberties and a parliamentary process, but the Tsar soon after went back on his word and limited the power of the Duma, leading to increased civil unreast.

Chapter Quiz

Ready to see how well you retained what you just read? Scan the QR code to go directly to the chapter quiz interface for this study guide. If you're using a computer, simply visit the online resources page at **mometrix.com/resources719/abcteworldhist** and click the Chapter Quizzes link.

World History 1914 to the Present

Entangling Alliances Prior to WWI

In the early years of the 20th century, relations among the various European powers were complex. Ever since the **Franco-Prussian War**, won by Prussia, the two sides had been enemies. At the center of their conflict was the territory of **Alsace-Lorraine**, which each side claimed as its own. In order to bolster their position in the region, each side entered into networks of alliances. After years of negotiations, two main alliances contained the major European powers: the **Triple Alliance** (Germany, Austria, Italy) and the **Triple Entente** (France, Britain, Russia). These two alliances would end up being the opposing sides in the great war of the ensuing years.

The Balkans and Beginning of WWI

In the years before the First World War, the **Balkans** were attempting to gain independence from the Hapsburg empire of Austria. This insurrection culminated in the assassination of Austrian **Archduke Franz Ferdinand** in 1914 by **Gavrilo Princip**, a member of a Serbian nationalist group. At this point, a chain reaction of war declarations (spurred by the comprehensive alliances of the time) ensued. Austria declared war against Serbia, Germany and Turkey joined with the Austrians, Russia declared war on these countries in support of Serbia, France joined with Russia, and Britain and Italy joined forces with France, even though Italy had been a member of the Triple Alliance.

Combat and Exit of Russia During WWI

Despite the fact that almost every nation in Europe had entered into World War I, most Europeans thought the conflict would be brief. Instead, advances in **weapons technology** made the war bloody and excruciatingly slow. Much of the fighting was done from **trenches**, and some battles would see the deaths of thousands of soldiers at a time. The war was also slow because the sides were very evenly matched; that is, until 1917, when the United States entered on the side of Britain. Also, in 1917, the Russians exited the war via the **Brest-Litovsk Treaty**. Russia was basically exhausted after suffering through a Revolution in 1917 in which the **Bolsheviks** came to power. The entry of the US provided the British and French with supplies and troops, and Germany was soon forced to call for a truce.

Treaty of Versailles

As the First World War wound down, a disgruntled German populace ousted the emperor and installed a moderate socialist government. This government, known as the **Weimar Republic**, would last until 1933. At the **Paris Peace Conference**, the victors of the war (the US, Britain, France, and Italy) exacted some revenge on Germany. The **Treaty of Versailles** penalized Germany economically and territorially; Alsace-Lorraine became independent, and the German military was dismantled. The Treaty of Versailles would need to be modified by two subsequent agreements: the **Treaty of Locarno,** which outlined a more reasonable reparations plan for Germany, and the **Kellogg-Briand Pact,** which asserted that diplomacy rather than force would be used to resolve conflicts.

Western Europe and Italy After the First World War

In the years after the First World War, the general mood in Europe was one of wariness. Most nations were exhausted by the conflict, and few felt that the signing of the **Treaty of Versailles** and the formation of the **League of Nations** had created a permanent peace. In the 1920s, Britain, Germany, France, and the United States were all liberal democracies without a strong executive. Unlike the United States, however, the European nations suffered a profound economic depression.

One nation that saw no diminution in nationalism was **Italy**. In part out of a fear of communism, Italians supported the rise of the fascist dictator **Benito Mussolini**. **Fascism** is defined as an extreme-right movement characterized by totalitarian rule with an emphasis on national unity and identity. Fascism generally manifests in dictatorial rule and suppression of the free speech and rights of dissenters. It originated in Italy and promised to the Italians a return to the glory days of Rome, when they were a mighty power ruled by a dominating executive. Of course, in order to maintain his authority, Mussolini had to brutally suppress any opposition.

Russian Revolution of 1917

After the **Revolution of 1905**, Russia had enjoyed a few years of relative peace. After a while, however, the peasants became dissatisfied with the weakness of the Duma, and after strikes and protests, **Czar Nicholas II** was forced to abdicate the throne. In place of the monarchy, a **provisional government** was set up to work alongside more progressive local councils, known as **Soviets**. These two groups were constantly at odds, however, especially during Russia's participation in the **First World War** (the Soviets wanted to withdraw and focus on national issues, while the Provisional Government felt obliged to fight). During this period, **Vladimir Lenin** rose to prominence as the Marxist leader of the **Bolshevik Party**. In the **Russian Revolution of 1917**, Lenin and his supporters ousted the provisional government and exited the war. Lenin then began the immense project of nationalizing the Soviet economy.

Lenin and Stalin

After his success in the Revolution of 1917, **Lenin** began to advocate the revolt of the working class in other nations. Naturally, this did not endear the new Russian government to the leaders of other nations. Russia became increasingly isolated both economically and politically from the rest of the world. Domestically, Lenin established the **New Economic Policy**, which blended capitalism and communism. This plan worked well enough in agriculture, but it never achieved much success in industry. After Lenin's death, **Joseph Stalin** came to power and began an ambitious plan of collectivizing farms and nationalizing factories (known as the **Five Year Plans**). Stalin was ruthless in the pursuit of his goals; he established labor camps to house his opponents. It is estimated that 20 million people were killed by Stalin's regime during the period now known as the **Great Terror**.

China in the Early 20h Century

In 1911, the **Manchu dynasty**, which had been significantly weakened by the **Boxer Rebellion**, was finally overthrown. A period of instability followed, in which **Sun Yat-sen** declared the creation of a republic with its headquarters in Nanking. Sun Yat-sen began a political party aimed at improving life for the common people; it was known as the **Kuomintang**. During this period, both Mongolia and Tibet declared their independence from China. The Chinese people became disenchanted with the Kuomintang government after what they saw as unfavorable agreements following World War I. After the death of Sun Yat-sen in 1925, a national government was established at Canton; the **communist party** was a major participant in this government.

Rule of the Kuomintang and the Sino-Japanese War in 20th-Century China

In 1926, the military leader **Chiang Kai-shek** led campaigns in central and northern China, in the hopes of unifying the country. During this period, Chiang broke with the **communist party**, and Communists were persecuted in Shanghai. In 1927, a national government led by the **Kuomintang**, who had previously fallen out of favor, was established in Nanking. The peasants were not pleased with this leadership, and they were organized as the **Red Army** under **Mao Tse-tung** in the south. In what is known as the **Long March**, Mao led his army north to Yenan, where they would gather strength. The situation in China was made even more volatile by the Japanese invasion in 1937. In what is known as the "**Rape of Nanking**," Japanese troops killed over 200,000 Chinese. The people were outraged, and the partisan splits between Mao's communists and Chiang's government only widened.

Japan in the Years Before WWII

In 1926, amid growing nationalism, **Hirohito** became the Emperor of Japan. The next year, the Japanese prime minister declared that Japan should dominate Asia, and four years later, Japanese forces invaded **Manchuria**. Some historians consider this to be the beginning of the Second World War. After establishing a puppet regime in Manchuria, the Japanese withdrew from the League of Nations and attacked China. The **Sino-Japanese War** ensued. In 1938, Japan outlined its new vision of **Co-Prosperity Spheres**; Japan would be the industrial center of Asia and would acquire its raw materials from its colonies in the rest of Asia. Japan promoted this idea as an opportunity to break from European imperialism, but it was really just the substitution of one master for another. In 1940, Japan would complete its transformation into a **fascist state** by dissolving all political parties.

Events Leading to World War II in Europe

Still shell-shocked from the First World War, the nations of western Europe were slow to respond to the growing menace of **Nazi Germany**. In general, they pursued a policy of appeasement and isolation. The British prime minister **Neville Chamberlain** was especially committed to using diplomacy over war. Then, in 1936, Hitler sent troops to occupy the **Rhineland**, a strip of territory on the German border. At around the same time, **Mussolini** invaded Ethiopia; the two aggressors, Germany and Italy, entered into an agreement making them the **Axis Powers**. In 1938, Germany annexed Austria and indicated that it was about to attack Czechoslovakia. In response to these actions, Chamberlain brought together Mussolini and Hitler for the **Munich Conference of 1938**. These talks would only briefly suspend German aggression.

Weimar Republic and the Rise of Hitler

After the abdication of the emperor, Germany was ruled by a legislative body known as the **Weimar Republic**. Most Germans felt that this group had been too willing to accept punishment in the treaties that followed the war. Germans also thought that this government was responsible for the **inflation** which crippled the German economy in the post-war period. Germany, then, was vulnerable to the charms of a leader who told them they had nothing about which to be ashamed. This leader was **Adolf Hitler** (1889-1945). A failed artist, Hitler became the head of the **National Socialist**, or **Nazi**, party. His speeches were expressions of ardent nationalism, although often Hitler seemed to be calling for a return to an ideal German state that had never actually existed.

Belief System of the Nazi Party

Led by **Adolf Hitler**, the Nazi party championed the **Aryan race** as superior to all others, especially the "insidious" Jews. Hitler suggested that the noble ambitions of the true German people required ***lebensraum***, or living space. In other words, Germany needed more territory. In its early days, the Nazi party was part of the German republican system; Nazi candidates ran for office and served in the **Reichstag** (German parliament). As Germany suffered through a terrible economic depression in the early 1930s, however, the people became impatient. In 1933, the Reichstag was set on fire, and the Nazis used the opportunity to claim total control of the government. Hitler had already been appointed Chancellor in January 1933. He was able to quickly improve the German economy, mostly through the expansion of the weapon-building industry. At the same time, the new government began to quietly round up Jews, Gypsies, and homosexuals.

Holocaust

As **Germany** sank deeper and deeper into dire economic straits, the tendency was to look for a person or group of people to blame for the problems of the country. With distrust of the **Jewish**

people already ingrained, it was easy for German authorities to set up the Jews as scapegoats for Germany's problems.

The Holocaust is the name given to the systematic killing of Jews, Gypsies, homosexuals, and others by the Nazis. **Anti-Semitism** had existed in Europe for millennia, but the Nazis gave it renewed emphasis and, after making numerous false claims about Jews, began persecuting them upon Hitler's rise to power in 1933. Jews were disenfranchised, forced into ghettos, had their property taken, and were finally sent to work and be killed in **concentration camps**. Approximately 6 million Jews were killed during the **Holocaust**. As the situation for the Germans became more dire in the Second World War, Hitler sought to implement what he called the "final solution," in which hundreds of thousands were killed just before the fall of Nazi Germany.

The Allies were aware of rumors of mass slaughter throughout the war, but many discounted the reports. Only when troops went in to liberate the prisoners was the true horror of the concentration camps brought to light.

> **Review Video: The Holocaust**
> Visit mometrix.com/academy and enter code: 350695

Consequences of the Holocaust

Many of the Nazi leaders were tried and convicted at the **Nuremberg trials** for their roles in the Holocaust. West Germany would later issue a **Federal Compensation Law**, through which billions of dollars were paid to survivors. During and after the Holocaust, Zionist Jews fled to **Palestine**. Public sympathy with their plight would be one of the main reasons for the creation of **Israel** in 1948. The total destruction of the Jewish community in Europe caused many Jews to question their faith, and those that remained in Europe are markedly more secular than their ancestors. The shock of the Holocaust has also caused many institutions, including the Roman Catholic Church, to consider their own latent anti-Semitism. Unfortunately, the anti-genocide legislation created in response to the Holocaust was not strict enough to rally international support against the **Rwandans** (who slaughtered hundreds of thousands of Tutsis in 1994) or the **Bosnian Serbs and Croats** (who killed thousands of Muslims in the early 1990s).

Pacific Arena in WWII

The **Japanese**, like the Germans, became seduced by the notion of their own racial superiority during the 1930s. As in Germany, this inevitably led to a lust for territorial expansion. By 1941, Japan had conquered Korea, Manchuria, and parts of China. Japan was also threatening to invade American interests in the Philippines. The United States imposed **economic sanctions** on Japan, making it difficult for the Japanese war industry to function. In response, the Japanese launched a surprise attack on the United States by bombing the US naval base of **Pearl Harbor**. After the attack on Pearl Harbor, the United States declared war upon Japan (and Germany, in turn, declared war on the United States). The Japanese made huge territorial gains before the US turned the tide at the **Battles of Midway and Guadalcanal**. The war in the Pacific would take much longer than the war in Europe due to the island-hopping nature of the fight. The unwillingness of the Japanese to surrender made it almost impossible for America to entirely vanquish them without enormous loss of life. So, the United States decided to drop atomic bombs on **Hiroshima** and **Nagasaki** to force Japan to surrender and finally end the war in the Pacific in August 1945.

Beginning and Initial Years of World War II in Europe

After **Chamberlain** had tried to forestall German aggression at the **Munich Conference of 1938**, Germany nevertheless invaded Czechoslovakia in 1939. It was also during this year that Hitler signed a secret agreement with **Stalin** pledging not to attack Russia so long as Russia stayed out of German affairs. Hitler then declared war on and conquered Poland. At this step, Great Britain and France were finally forced to declare war upon Germany. Germany at this point was a dominating military adversary. New advances in motorized military vehicles made it possible for Germany to conquer large areas of land quickly in a new form of warfare called **Blitzkrieg** (lightning war). The **Axis powers** conquered almost the entire European continent, including France, over the course of 1940. Only Great Britain remained in opposition, and the Nazis undertook a ferocious aerial assault on the British, who were by then led by **Winston Churchill**, but failed to do enough damage to make an invasion of the island country practical. Instead, Hitler turned east and decided to violate his truce with Stalin, invading **Russia** in 1941. The Germans overwhelmed much of the Soviet military and advanced deep into Russian territory in a huge surprise offensive.

Middle Years and Conclusion of World War II in Europe

The tide turned against Hitler once the United States entered the war. The harsh Russian winter halted the German advance into Russia short of Moscow in 1941. The Germans made further gains in the summer of 1942 but were decisively beaten at the **Battle of Stalingrad** and were slowly pushed back out of Russia from then on. American and British troops landed in North Africa in 1942 and used that as a springboard to invade Italy in 1943. In 1944, the Americans and British opened yet another front with a massive invasion of northern France in the **D-Day landings**. Fighting numerically superior forces on multiple fronts, the Germans steadily lost ground and the Allies pushed into Germany from both East and West in 1945. Surrounded and with the war lost, Hitler committed **suicide** in his bunker in Berlin in April 1945, and the remaining German forces **surrendered** shortly afterward.

India and Pakistan After WWII

In 1947, after years of peaceful protests led by **Mahatma Gandhi**, India was given its independence and partitioned into two states, **India** and **Pakistan**. The following year, Gandhi would be assassinated in India. In 1965, border disputes would flare into the **Indo-Pakistani War**. In 1971, Pakistan would fend off attacks from Bengali rebels, who sought to achieve independence. The next year, however, **Bangladesh** would be established as an independent state. In 1984, India had its own internal problems; after the Indian army occupied the **Golden Temple** sacred to the Sikhs, the Indian leader **Indira Gandhi** was assassinated by her Sikh bodyguards. **Anti-Sikh riots** resulted, and much blood was shed.

Beginnings of The Cold War

After the defeat of the Axis powers in WWII, the United States and Russia entered into a long and often secret conflict, in which each side used diplomatic, economic, and occasionally military forces to try to assert itself as the dominant world power. The first issue on which these nations butted heads was the **rebuilding of Europe**. Germany was divided into an eastern and western section; the western half was democratic and looked to the US for guidance, while Eastern Germany became a communist nation in the USSR's sphere of influence. Russia worked to bring all of its neighbors (including Poland, Czechoslovakia, Hungary, Romania, and Bulgaria) under its control. The western borders of these nations formed what Churchill referred to as the **iron curtain**, dividing communist Eastern Europe from democratic Western Europe.

Truman Doctrine, Marshall Plan, NATO, and Warsaw Pact

In order to stop the spread of communism in Europe and elsewhere, President Truman asserted his policy of "containment" in the so-called **Truman Doctrine**. This meant that the US would support the anticommunist governments throughout the world. The **Marshall Plan** advanced this policy by supplying aid to war-ravaged countries in Western Europe. When the **Eastern Bloc countries** prevented aid from reaching West Berlin, the US, England, and France organized the **Berlin Airlift** to overcome this obstacle. In 1949, the Western European and North American nations entered into a mutual defense treaty, NATO (North Atlantic Treaty Organization). As a response, the Eastern Bloc nations joined with the Soviet Union in the **Warsaw Pact**.

Communist Revolution in China

China was torn by civil strife all throughout the Second World War. At one point, the American government had to renounce its trade rights in **China** in order to persuade China not to sign a peace treaty with Japan while the US still needed Chinese support. Once Japan had been defeated, the **Red Army** under Mao moved into **Manchuria** (which had recently been vacated by the Soviets). The major cities were still occupied by Nationalist forces, supported by the Americans. In 1946, fighting resumed between the opposing factions, and the **Nationalists** under Chiang were eventually forced to abandon central China. In 1949, the Red Army forced Chiang Kai-shek to leave the mainland and find refuge in Taiwan. On October 1, 1949, the communists declared the official creation of the **People's Republic of China**.

Arms Race, Cuban Missile Crisis, and Bay of Pigs in the Cold War

During the **Cold War**, the United States and the Soviet Union each tried to deter an attack by the other by building up fantastic arsenals of **nuclear missiles**. The two nations would also expend considerable effort trying to be the first in space. Finally, in the late 60s and early 70s, the two nations would begin talks aimed at mutual disarmament. This occurred in part because relations between China and the USSR had cooled. Before this period of détente, however, there had been a couple of serious threats to global peace. In 1961, the US had financed an unsuccessful invasion of Cuba at the **Bay of Pigs**. This led the Soviet Union to establish missile bases on communist Cuba; the US and USSR almost declared war on one another during the **Cuban Missile Crisis of 1962**.

End of the Cold War

Over time, the leaders of the Soviet Union and United States began to realize the total annihilation that would ensue if nuclear war was declared, and it was agreed that both sides would **disarm**. The two treaties that were signed during the 1970s are known as the **Strategic Arms Limitation Talks (SALT) I and II**. When **Mikhail Gorbachev** came into power in the USSR in 1985, he established a policy of **glasnost**, or "openness." In response to US President Ronald Reagan's military build-up using the might of the US economy, Gorbachev understood that the Soviet Union could not economically compete militarily under a communist system and overcome the military might of the United States. He thus advocated **perestroika**, a gradual metamorphosis of the Soviet economy. In 1991, these reforms culminated in the disintegration of the ruling Communist party, and the **disbanding of the Soviet Union**. This occurred two years after the **Berlin Wall**, which for more than forty years had separated communist and anticommunist Germany, was finally torn down.

Review Video: The End of the Cold War
Visit mometrix.com/academy and enter code: 278032

Middle East from 1947 to 1977

After WWII, the United Nations announced that **Palestine** would be partitioned in order to make room for a new Jewish state. **Israel** was created in 1948. In 1951, the Iranian leader **Mossadegh** nationalized the oil interests, making his government extremely wealthy and powerful. This move would be emulated by future leaders. In 1967, in the **Six-Day War**, Israel routed a coalition of Arab nations, seizing the West Bank, Sinai, and Jerusalem. In 1972, Palestinian terrorists murdered 12 Israeli athletes at the Olympics in Munich. In 1973, the oil-producing Arab nations placed an embargo on shipments to the West, causing major energy crises in the US and Europe. Also, in 1973,

Israelis and Arabs battled again in the **Yom Kippur War**. In 1977, Egyptian leader **Anwar Sadat** became the first Arab leader to visit Israel.

Middle East from 1978 to 1985

In 1978, American President **Jimmy Carter** hosted successful peace talks between Egypt and Israel at **Camp David**. The next year, however, a fundamentalist Islamist regime would take power in Iran, and many Americans would be taken hostage, only released upon the election of **Ronald Reagan**. Between 1980 and 1988, Iran and Iraq engaged in a bloody and brutal war, begun when the Iraqi leader **Saddam Hussein** seized territory in eastern Iran. Also, during this period, Afghan rebels were engaged in a prolonged, ultimately successful fight for independence from the Soviets. In 1982, Israel attacked Lebanon, which was harboring the Palestinian leader **Yasser Arafat**. Lebanon would be forced to oust Arafat the next year. Israel would continue attacking Arafat and the **Palestinian Liberation Organization**, and the PLO would continue to sponsor terrorist activities against Israel.

Middle East from 1987 to 2003

In 1987, Syrian troops entered Lebanon and stopped the civil war. Also, during this year, 402 pilgrims died during riots in the Saudi Arabian sacred city of Mecca. In 1988, the Palestinian resistance (known as the Intifada) began in earnest against Israel. Iraq invaded Kuwait in 1990, and after UN sanctions were levied, the US invaded in 1991. The Iraqi soldiers set fire to thousands of Kuwaiti oil wells while retreating. In 1992, Arafat and Israeli PM Yitzhak Rabin shook hands in Washington, and Arafat would soon return to Gaza after years of exile. In 1995, the Israelis and Palestinians signed an agreement giving the Palestinians autonomy in the West Bank and Gaza areas. Despite continuing violence, another agreement was reached in 1998, this one stating that the Palestinians would be granted land in exchange for keeping the peace. Violence continued, however, and in 2003, Israel began construction of a barrier between itself and the Palestinian territories.

New Europe after 1991 through 1998

In 1991, **Gorbachev** resigned as the last president of the USSR, and a number of the Soviet provinces, including Lithuania and Latvia, declared independence. The **Maastricht Treaty**, formally announcing the creation of the European Union, was signed in 1992, and the next year a unified European stock market opened. In the **"Velvet" Revolution of 1993**, Slovakia separated from Czechoslovakia, which became the Czech Republic. Meanwhile, the former USSR was enduring civil strife until **Boris Yeltsin** seized power in 1993. In 1994, Russian troops attacked **Chechnya**, which was trying to achieve independence. In 1998, President Clinton helped broker a peace agreement between the **British** and **North Irish rebels**.

New Europe After 1999

In 1999, the Czech Republic, Poland, and Hungary all joined **NATO**, further eliminating the old divides between western and eastern Europe. The conflict in Chechnya increased during this year, and Yeltsin was succeeded as Russian leader by the former KGB agent Vladimir Putin. An **International Criminal Court** was created in the Hague (Netherlands) in 2002, despite the vehement opposition of the United States. In the late '90s, many of the western European governments had become quasi-socialist, and they spent much of their time debating the immense increase in **immigration**. Meanwhile, the former Soviet states have had a rough transition from command to market economies, and are still somewhat economically depressed.

Emergence of the Pacific Rim After 1991

In the 1990s and early years of the 21st century, Japan and China emerged as two major economic powers. Despite suffering a prolonged recession, **Japan** continued to be one of the world's manufacturing leaders. However, several internal scandals have shaken Japanese confidence and have caused many to question the close relations between corporations and government. In **China**, the suffocating communist regime has relaxed its economic strictures somewhat, and the result has been an economic boom. China created several **special economic zones** along its eastern coast to lure foreign business. Now however, Chinese firms are control a sizable portion of the market in their own right.

First World, Second World, and Third World

First-world nations are those that have advanced capitalist economies and are fully industrialized. The former Soviet states, which are slowly developing capitalist economies after having inefficient socialist economies for so long, are classified as **second-world nations**. This term has fallen out of general use, as these nations have slowly become more similar to first-world nations. The relatively poor and non-industrialized nations of Latin America, Africa, and Asia, most of which were colonized or involved in other exploitative trade arrangements with the Western empires at one time, are known as the **third-world nations**. Although these nations are far more numerous than those of the first or second world, they wield much less political power.Underdevelopment

Third-world countries that do not have the modern economic conditions possessed by the wealthier nations are said to suffer from **underdevelopment**. That is, they do not have the industrial, social, or political strength that is required to be a self-sustaining party in the global economy. In some countries, underdevelopment is clearly the result of **dysfunctional politics**; third-world nations are more likely to be ruled by a small group or by a dictator. Underdeveloped nations are typically those that were colonized at one time. Because their economy during the colonial period was so heavily based upon exporting raw materials, they never created a manufacturing base and found themselves unequipped for independence. Experts are at odds as to whether first-world nations should aid underdeveloped countries by funneling money to them or by helping them to develop modern economies.

Specific Technological Advances Since 1991

In 1993, the first **web browser** was developed, beginning the era of internet communications that has revolutionized every area of human life. The internet did not become widely used, however, until 1997 and 1998. In 1997, a Scottish lab successfully **cloned** a lamb from adult sheep DNA, opening the door to the cloning of other animals, or human organs for medical purposes, and even for the cloning of entire human beings. This last possibility was strengthened in 2001, when the work of **sequencing the DNA** of the human genome was finally finished. Although **embryonic stem-cell research** has been limited in the US (other sources than embryos remain legal), other countries are using cells from human embryos to search for cures for disease. Another leap in genetic technology came in 2012 with the advent of CRISPR, a tool for directly editing the genes of any organism. In 2008, a new technology was used to implement Bitcoin called blockchain. This is a powerful method for sharing and storing information in an incredibly secure way, among many other uses. One of the most astonishing acheivements in science in recent history was in 2016 when the LIGO observatory used incredibly sensitive detectors to sense gravitational waves from distant colliding black holes.

Modernization

Modernization is the process by which societies develop sophisticated industrial technology, as well as the political, cultural, and social systems that are most effective in sustaining and advancing that technology. For a long time, sociologists noted that the most modernized countries, namely the Western empires, were the most successful, and that other societies should strive to emulate them. In recent decades, however, more sensitive sociologists have declared that **modernization** need not be equated with Westernization, and that the indigenous cultures of South America and Africa, for example, need not be cast off for these places to enjoy prosperity. One way sociologists can assess the relative modernization of a society is by comparing the **gross national product** (GNP), which is the total value of all economic activity within a society. Often, GNP is divided by total population to determine a society's **per capita gross national product**.

State Theory of Modernization and World System Theory of Modernization

The state theory of modernization supports the ideals of **capitalism** by maintaining that whenever the government is restricted from seizing private property, capitalism will develop and free markets will arise as people modernize and strive to become more productive. The **world system theory of modernization**, also known as the **dependency theory**, states that some nations modernize at the expense of less-developed nations, and that so long as this exploitation continues, the less-developed nations will be unable to improve their lot. This theory essentially takes the **Marxist** view of the capitalist society, in which those who own the means of production are able to maintain dominance over the workers, and applies it to the interactions of nations.

Globalization

Globalization is the process whereby all the social groups in the world are being brought into closer connection with one another. This has occurred mainly through the advances in transportation and communication technology, although the era of colonialism also had the effect of shrinking the world. This phenomenon has, in some cases, made it more difficult for repressive regimes to isolate themselves; during the Tiananmen Square uprising in China, for instance, Western media was able to communicate with the student rebels and present their story to the rest of the world. Many observers lament **globalization**, however, because they feel it will homogenize culture and crowd out fascinating, but not economically successful, societies.

Review Video: Globalization
Visit mometrix.com/academy and enter code: 551962

Automation

Automation is when machines are employed to do work formerly done by humans. This is typically done when an industry seeks to have greater worker productivity, but it may have some costly side effects. The work that remains for people after automation is frequently repetitive and mindless. Sociologists studying the phenomenon have observed increased alienation and lowered self-esteem among workers whose jobs have been automated. Also, automation reduces the need for specialization by driving employees out of their previously unique fields; this creates both unhealthy competition for menial jobs and confusion over social roles among the workers. Unfortunately, the pressures of the **capitalist market** make it impossible for most businesses to avoid automation.

Hyperurbanization

Hyperurbanization has occurred when the development of population growth in urban areas has moved too quickly and has outpaced the necessary accompanying growths in industry and business. The inevitable result of **hyperurbanization** is unemployment and inadequate public services. This has been a particular problem in **third-world countries**, which are experiencing mass internal migration from the countryside to the cities. In fact, the urbanization currently taking place in China may be the largest movement of people in the history of the world. It is impossible for any society, no matter how wealthy, to keep up with such a migration and provide adequate roads, health care, education, water, food, and electricity.

Chapter Quiz

Ready to see how well you retained what you just read? Scan the QR code to go directly to the chapter quiz interface for this study guide. If you're using a computer, simply visit the online resources page at **mometrix.com/resources719/abcteworldhist** and click the Chapter Quizzes link.

ABCTE World History Practice Test

Want to take this practice test in an online interactive format?
Check out the online resources page, which includes interactive practice questions and much more: **mometrix.com/resources719/abcteworldhist**

1. Which of the following is not a common characteristic of all early civilizations?

a. Agricultural surplus.
b. Clear division of labor.
c. A pictographic writing system.
d. Population centers such as towns and cities.
e. Some form of government.

2. Which of the following rivers did NOT play an important role in the development of the earliest civilizations?

a. The Tiber River.
b. The Yangtze River.
c. The Euphrates River.
d. The Nile River.
e. The Indus River.

3. "The river was easy to navigate because of a peculiar trait: Its strong winds blew in the opposite direction of its water's flow. The winds blew down from the north, but the river flowed up from the south. This unusual feature made it easy to transport goods back and forth from the Mediterranean Sea, which lay to the north.

Which river is most likely being described in the above passage?

a. The Tiber River.
b. The Tigris River.
c. The Nile Rivers.
d. The Yangtze River.
e. The Indus River.

4. Which of the following rulers was female?

a. Sargon.
b. Hammurabi.
c. Hatshepsut.
d. Nebuchadnezzar.
e. Amenhotep IV.

5. "Because of the central role religion played in Sumerian culture, priests held much of the real power, despite the existence of a king. Beneath them a class of warrior nobles, responsible for protecting the city, held the next level of power. Less powerful than the nobles but still influential were the lower priests, scholars, and merchants who took responsibility for many of the daily operations of the government."

Which characteristic of most early civilizations does this passage reflect?

a. Agricultural surplus.
b. Population centers
c. Religious practice.
d. Development of technology
e. Government.

6. In what modern-day country are the remains of the Mesopotamian civilization found?

a. Afghanistan
b. Iraq
c. Türkiye
d. Egypt
e. Lebanon

7. "The king allowed the conquered the right to maintain their own religious practices, local laws, and customs. This practice, however, shares no similarities with our present-day principals of tolerance. In effect, allowing conquered people to maintain their own religions and customs forged a bond of loyalty between the conqueror and the conquered. Though the conquered preserved many rights and customs, local governors called Satraps, along with a network of spies, maintained order and reported back to the King."

Which empire does the above passage describe?

a. Persians.
b. Akkadians.
c. Babylonians.
d. Egyptians.
e. Sumerians.

8. A monotheistic religious practice was central to which of the following cultures?

a. Egyptians.
b. Hebrews.
c. Sumerians.
d. Babylonians.
e. Hittites.

9. Which of the following is a character from the *Epic of Gilgamesh*?

a. Ahura Mazda.
b. Enkidu.
c. Yahweh.
d. Thoth.
e. Zoroaster.

10. According to tradition, who founded the Israelite people?

a. Zoroaster.
b. Abraham.
c. Aeneas.
d. Daniel.
e. Jesus.

11. Which of the following was NOT developed by the Phoenicians?

a. Purple dye.
b. Sailing technology.
c. The alphabet.
d. Metalworking.
e. The ziggurat.

12. The first coin-based economy was established by which of the following people?

a. Phoenicians.
b. Egyptians.
c. Hebrews.
d. Lydians.

13. Which of the following statements is NOT true of Minoan culture?

a. The name honors King Minos.
b. Its capital was in Knossos on the island of Crete.
c. Minoan culture was overtaken by the Athenians.
d. Its capital was a maze-like structure of many chambers.
e. Much of our knowledge of Minoan culture comes from reconstructed wall paintings.

14. The word democracy comes from two Greek root words meaning what?

a. People and rule.
b. People and vote.
c. City and state.
d. Tyrant and overthrow.
e. People and freedom.

15. Which of the following refers to the slave class of ancient Sparta?

a. Helots.
b. Hoplites.
c. Ephorate.
d. Metics.
e. Archon.

16. What was the Athenian Draco known for?

a. His severely punitive legal system.
b. His great reforms of the legal system.
c. Leading Athenians into defeat in Sicily.
d. Incurring the resentment of other city-states by amassing too much power.
e. His comedic plays.

17. Which of the following was NOT a significant event in the Persian Wars?

a. Persia invaded the Greek mainland.
b. Persians were driven back at the Battle of Marathon.
c. The Greek forces vastly outnumbered the Persians.
d. The Persians attacked Athens.
e. Athens and Sparta unified their forces to defeat the Persians.

18. Which of the following is NOT an event associated with the golden age of Pericles?

a. Philosophy flourished under thinkers such as Socrates.
b. The Acropolis was reconstructed.
c. Many great plays were written and performed by tragedians such as Aeschylus and Sophocles.
d. The Iliad and Odyssey were written.
e. The study of history flourished under such historians as Herodotus and Thucydides.

19. Which of these factors did not contribute to the escalation of the Peloponnesian Wars?

a. Athens had amassed great power, which threatened other Greek city-states.
b. Athens had created a monopoly on sea trade in the region.
c. Several city-states formed an alliance with Sparta to keep Athens's power in check.
d. Athens invaded Sparta.
e. The Spartans invaded Attica, near Athens, in 431 B.C.

20. Which of the following statements are not true of BOTH the Iliad and the Odyssey?

a. Both deal with the Trojan War or its aftermaths.
b. Both focus primarily on the character Odysseus.
c. Both are attributed to a poet named Homer.
d. Both were written around 700 B.C.
e. Both were based on an oral tradition of bards reciting poems to audiences.

21. Who is the Greek goddess of war?

a. Aphrodite.
b. Hera.
c. Athena.
d. Demeter.
e. Artemis.

22. "In the 5th Century B.C., the most popular career choice for intelligent young Greek males was politics. To prepare children for life as a politician, many parents hired travelling teachers to instruct young pupils in such skills as rhetoric, politics, grammar, and history. The name for these educators derives from the Greek word for 'wisdom.'"

Who are the teachers described in the above passage?

a. Philosophers.
b. Sophists.
c. Rhetoricians.
d. Orators.
e. Politicians.

23. Which of the following statements about women in ancient Athens are not true?

a. Many female infants were abandoned or killed.
b. Women stayed in the home to manage servants and raise young children.
c. Women were allowed to vote, but their vote did not count as much as men's.
d. Women could not hold public office.
e. Women could not inherit property.

24. Which nation eventually overtook ancient Greece?

a. Persia.
b. Macedon.
c. Egypt.
d. Syria.
e. India.

25. Which of the following explanations accounts for the spread of Hellenism, i.e. Greek culture, in the decades following the overthrow of Greek power?

a. Many countries voluntarily adopted Greek government and culture because it was superior to their own.
b. Greek soldiers took control of the Persian Empire, imposing Greek culture on all of Persia's former conquests.
c. The spread of Hellenism was stopped after the overthrow of Greek power.
d. Rome was influenced by Greek culture and spread its version of Hellenism as it amassed power and territory.
e. Alexander, ruler of Macedon, adopted Greek culture as his own and spread it throughout the ancient world.

26. Which of the following statements are not true of Alexander the Great?

a. Alexander conquered Persia in 336 B.C.
b. Alexander took control of Egypt and founded Alexandria in 331 B.C.
c. Alexander conquered all of India.
d. Alexander's conquests ended after his troops mutinied.
e. Alexander died in 323 B.C. at the age of 33.

27. Which of the statements below is not true of the century following the death of Alexander?

a. Alexander's generals began fighting for control over the empire.
b. Alexander's brother took power only to be executed.
c. Alexander's heir took power and was executed.
d. Alexander's son brought peace to the empire and ushered in the Golden Age of Hellenistic Culture.
e. The generals divided the conquered lands into separate kingdoms and waged war with each other.

28. Which statement is closest to the core beliefs of the Greeks?

a. "Seize the day."
b. "Everything in moderation."
c. "Do unto others as you would have them do unto you."
d. "Live and let live."
e. "An eye for an eye."

29. Which of these statements does not reflect an influence on Greek art?

a. The symmetry of Greek sculpture and architecture shows the influence of geometry and mathematics.
b. Sculptures of bodies in motion show the Greek admiration of athletic skill.
c. The expressions of humility on the faces of statues reflect the belief that all humanity is fallen from grace.
d. The popularity of vases and pottery shows Greeks valued functionality as well as beauty.
e. The simple designs of Greek art reflect their distaste for excess and their praise of moderation.

30. Our primary source of knowledge about the philosophy of Socrates was preserved in what way?

a. On stone tablets he composed.
b. In the writings of his students.
c. On scrolls of papyrus he composed.
d. In comedic plays that depict his life.
e. In works written hundreds of years after his death.

31. "This school of thought held that certainty is an illusion because no knowledge can be absolutely true. The universe constantly changes, and what is true for one time is not true for all. Thinkers who followed this school's founder, Pyrrho, questioned all scientific and religious beliefs."

The above passage reflects which of the following school of thought?

a. Skepticism.
b. Epicureanism.
c. Cynicism.
d. Stoicism.
e. Dualism.

32. "They are indestructible, constantly in motion, indivisible, and infinite. All material substances are composed of them. This theory of atoms is remarkable in that it anticipates scientific theories that would be confirmed two and a half millennia later."

Which of the following Greek philosophers is primarily responsible for the ideas described in the above passage?

a. Socrates.
b. Aristotle.
c. Plato.
d. Thales.
e. Democritus.

33. Which of the following statements about Greek contribution to modern science is not true?

a. Aristotle was one of the first to explore the fields we now know as comparative anatomy, taxonomy, and embryology.
b. Socrates was the first to argue that the material world is composed of indivisible units called atoms.
c. Hippocrates separated the study of medicine from religion and was one of the first to establish effective medical theories.
d. Herophilus dissected cadavers to advance the field of human anatomy.
e. Euclid established many of the foundations of the study of geometry.

34. The three works by Aeschylus, *Agamemnon, Libation Bearers,* and *Eumenides* make up the only surviving trilogy of Greek drama known as

a. The Oresteia.
b. The Oedipus Trilogy.
c. The Iliad.
d. The Odyssey.
e. The Antigone Trilogy.

35. Which of the following events was the central focus of Herodotus' work, The *Histories*?

a. The Persian invasion of the Greek mainland.
b. The infiltration of Troy by soldiers hidden in a wooden horse.
c. Sparta's defeat of Athens.
d. King Oedipus' realization that he had married his own mother.
e. The murder of Agamemnon.

36. "He was one of Socrates' star pupils who went on to found the Academy in Athens to teach philosophy. He preferred to express his ideas in dramatic dialog, a style that often makes it hard to determine the exact point of view he promoted. Among his best known arguments is the theory of forms, which argues that the world we experience is an imperfect reflection of a higher, idealized realm."

The above passage refers to which famous Greek philosopher?

a. Aristotle.
b. Thales.
c. Anaxagoras.
d. Parmenides.
e. Plato.

37. Which of the following statements about the education of wealthy Athenian males is false?

a. Children attended group schools where they studied reading, writing, poetry, and grammar.
b. Children were taken out of their homes and placed in a grueling public education program designed to build physical and psychological endurance.
c. Children studied sports such as gymnastics, javelin throwing, and boxing.
d. Adolescents studied government, ethics, mathematics, and rhetoric in the schools of the Sophists.
e. Eighteen-year olds were obligated to spend one year in military service.

38. Which group overtook Rome in the mid-600s BC and established much of its infrastructure, including sewers, roads, and fortifications, only to be driven out of the city in 509 BC?

a. Latins.
b. Etruscans.
c. Greeks.
d. Persians.
e. Mesopotamians.

39. Which of the following facts about the Latins is false?

a. Their culture was influenced by southern Italian tribes.
b. They established their first villages along the Tiber River.
c. They united to create the city of Rome around 300 A.D.
d. Their language became the language of the Roman Empire.
e. They took the city again after it had been occupied and rebuilt by a kingdom from the north.

40. "These men occupied the most powerful level of the Roman Republic. They were responsible for controlling the public treasury and foreign policy. Once appointed, they held the position for the remainder of their lives. They were even entitled to appoint a dictator for a six-month period in the event of an emergency."

Who does the above passage describe?

a. Senators.
b. Magistrates.
c. Praetors.
d. Censors.
e. Consuls.

41. Which of the following is not an effect of the Punic Wars between Rome and Carthage?

a. Over the course of the wars, Rome developed a powerful navy.
b. After suffering defeat in all three of the Punic Wars, Carthage was destroyed.
c. Rome emerged as the dominant power in the Mediterranean.
d. Carthage emerged more powerful than before the Punic Wars, becoming a serious threat to Roman power.
e. Macedonia lost its influence in the region.

42. The Conflict of the Orders was a dispute between

a. Rome and Carthage.
b. Rome and Macedonia.
c. The Latins, Greeks, and Etruscans.
d. Wealthy Roman landowners and the lower class Plebeians.
e. Rome and Sicily.

43. What caused the first Punic War in 246 B.C.?

a. Hannibal attacked Rome from the mountainous north.
b. The Romans destroyed Carthage and sold all its citizens into slavery.
c. Carthage intervened in a dispute between Rome and the island of Sicily.
d. Rome defeated Macedonia.
e. Roman forces attacked northern Africa.

44. What was the main reason Julius Caesar was assassinated in 44 B.C.?

a. He had removed himself to the Island of Capri to lead a life of depravity.
b. His political opponents believed he had amassed too much power.
c. He appointed his horse to the senate.
d. He led his armies in an attack against Rome.
e. He and Cleopatra attempted to attack Augustus at the Battle of Actium.

45. Who was not a member of the Julio-Claudian line of Roman Emperors?

a. Tiberius.
b. Claudius.
c. Caligula.
d. Nero.
e. Marcus Aurelius.

46. The "Good Emperors" who ruled Rome from 96 to 180 A.D. included:

a. Nerva, Trajan, Hadrian, Antoninus Pius, and Marcus Aurelius.
b. Tiberius Gracchus, Gaius Gracchus, Gaius Marius, and Lucius Cornelius Sulla.
c. Galba, Otho, and Vitellius.
d. Pertinax, Didius Julianus, Septimius Serverus, Pescennius Niger, and Clodius Albinus.
e. Augustus, Tiberius, Caligula, Claudius, and Nero.

47. "This era represents the golden age of the Roman Empire. For about 200 years, the Empire experienced relatively few attacks, stability among its conquered lands, and significant developments in architecture and the engineering of roads and bridges. This time period saw the greatest expansion of the empire and the Romanization of the western world."

The above passage refers to which era of Roman history?

a. The reign of Julio-Claudian line of emperors.
b. The reign of the Five Good Emperors.
c. Pax Romana.
d. The reign of the Flavian Emperors.
e. The era of the Gracchi.

48. Which of the following is not a major structure found in the city of Rome?

a. The Forum.
b. The Pantheon.
c. Hadrian's Wall.
d. The Colosseum.
e. House of the Vestal Virgins.

49. Led by Spartacus, the revolt in 73-71 B.C. reflects the disgruntlement of

a. The Praetorian Guard.
b. Senators.
c. Slaves.
d. Centuria.
e. The conquered provinces.

50. Which of the following did not make a significant contribution to Roman literature?

a. Horace.
b. Livy.
c. Plutarch.
d. Homer.
e. Virgil.

51. What did The *Metamorphoses* by the Roman poet Ovid describe?

a. The history of Greece.
b. The history of the Roman Republic.
c. Greek and Roman Myths.
d. The poet's advice for lovers.
e. The poet's family history.

52. To what do many historians attribute the Romans' preoccupation with bloodthirsty forms of entertainment such as gladiator battles and public executions?

a. High standard of living.
b. Pagan religious practices.
c. Moral decline.
d. Stoicism.
e. Economic decline.

53. "Before his religious conversion, he persecuted Jews who converted to Christianity. After experiencing a religious vision, he became the early Christian church's strongest proponent, founding and counseling churches throughout Greece and Macedonia. These churches went on to form the foundation of the religion that would eventually spread throughout the Roman Empire."

The above passage describes which of the men shown below?

a. Jesus.
b. Paul.
c. Peter.
d. David.
e. John.

54. Which of the following emperors made Christianity the official religion of the Roman Empire?

a. Theodosius.
b. Nero.
c. Marcus Aurelius.
d. Julius Caesar.
e. Hadrian.

55. Which of the following groups did not play a role in the Germanic invasions of Rome?

a. Ostrogoths.
b. Visigoths.
c. Vandals.
d. Huns.
e. Etruscans.

56. Which of the following factors did not lead to the split between the eastern and western Roman Empires?

a. Diocletian's decision to split the empire into two separate centers with authority divided between himself and a co-emperor.
b. Corruption and instability in the government.
c. The onset of the Crusades, a war between the eastern and western branches of the Christian Church.
d. Constantinople's emergence as a powerful city.
e. A widening gap between wealthy and impoverished citizens.

57. Which of the following statements does NOT describe Rome's relationship with its conquered peoples?

a. All subjects were granted the full range of rights entitled to Roman citizens.
b. The Romans allowed some degree of cultural autonomy.
c. Subjects were expected to follow Roman laws.
d. Subjects were obligated to pay taxes.
e. Subjects gave up land and supplies to the government.

58. In the 500s A.D., Byzantine emperor Justinian compiled the Justinian Code.

What does this code contain?

a. Roman laws and legal opinions.
b. The history of the Roman Emperors.
c. Roman religious practice.
d. Roman economic policies.
e. The great works of Roman literature.

59. What did the Iconoclasts oppose?

a. The elevation of religious leaders to powerful positions.
b. The use of religious images in worship.
c. The worship of saints.
d. The worship of the Mother Mary.
e. The watering-down of Christianity for the illiterate.

60. Which of the following is not one of the five pillars of Islam?

a. The profession of faith, "There is no god but Allah; Muhammad is the prophet of Allah."
b. The ritual of five daily prayers.
c. Payments made to provide for the poor and needy within a community.
d. One pilgrimage to holy city of Mecca in the Muslim's lifetime.
e. Abstinence from eating unclean animals.

61. This title meant "successor to the prophet" and was given to the main Islamic leaders who came to power after Mohammad's death.

a. Imam.
b. Caliph.
c. Sultan.
d. Sheik.
e. Vizier.

62. Which of the following scientific contributions was not made by Arabic thinkers?

a. The development of the Arabic numbering system.
b. The development of algebra.
c. Significant advances in trigonometry.
d. The invention of the abacus.
e. Advances in the use of decimals.

63. Which of the following events did not happen between 500 and 1000 A.D., the period known as the "Dark Ages"?

a. The fall of the Roman Empire.
b. The fragmentation of areas formally unified by Roman rule.
c. Cultural isolation due to the loss of dependable trade routes.
d. The global collapse of civilization.
e. Europe's loss of much of the knowledge advanced by Greek and Roman thinkers.

64. "His accomplishments include defeating the Lombards, Saxons, and Avars throughout Europe, deterring advances by Muslim armies in the Pyrenees Mountains, reviving Roman legal practice, increasing the strength of the Roman Catholic church, becoming the first Holy Roman Emperor of Europe, and establishing schools and libraries throughout Europe."

Who does the above passage describe?

a. Charlemagne.
b. Pope Leo III.
c. Charles Martel.
d. Clovis I.
e. Pepin II.

65. Under feudalism, this term refers to a person who controlled a large landholding and gave parts of it away in exchange for loyalty and protection.

a. Fief.
b. Homage.
c. Lord.
d. Primogeniture.
e. Vassal.

66. Which of the following statements is not true of manorialism?

a. The lord of a manor gave his land to serfs to cultivate.
b. The serfs kept just enough of the crops to sustain themselves but gave the majority to the lord.
c. Many serfs who worked diligently could become nobles.
d. Nobles lived apart from the serfs in a castle complex.
e. The serfs gave crops to the nobles in exchange for protection.

67. Which of the following statements is not true of the hierarchy of the Catholic Church?

a. Parish priests made up a diocese.
b. The head of the diocese was called a bishop.
c. The archdiocese was a collection of smaller dioceses overseen by the archbishop.
d. The curia was a group of archbishops with power over the pope.
e. The pope is the ultimate authority for the church.

68. Which of the following terms describes the practice of abolishing Catholics who did not believe in official church policies or doctrines?

a. Heretics.
b. Excommunication.
c. Interdict.
d. Canon Law.
e. Indulgences.

69. Which of the following held themselves to the code of chivalry?

a. Serfs.
b. Archbishops.
c. Troubadours.
d. Vassals.
e. Knights.

70. Which of the following statements best characterizes the work of Thomas Aquinas?

a. He attempted to use the logical techniques developed by Aristotle to justify belief in the divinity of Christ.
b. His Canterbury Tales was written in a vernacular language instead of Latin.
c. His Divine Comedy tells the story of a man's journey into hell, through purgatory, and onward to paradise.
d. His followers, the Franciscans, attempted to follow in the footsteps of Jesus, travelling and ministering while refusing financial compensation.
e. He believed that the church was like a "city of God" separate from the "city of man."

71. This organization helped protect the rights of workers who practiced a craft.

a. Charters.
b. Fief.
c. Manor.
d. Guilds.
e. Banks.

72. To what does the term "Black Death" refer?

a. Viking warfare in the 9th Century.
b. The plague that killed 25 million in the 1300s.
c. An execution method common in the feudal system.
d. Excommunication by the Catholic Church.
e. A form of combat used among knights.

73. Who were the Angles and Saxons?

a. Viking invaders of England.
b. Groups from French Normandy.
c. Members of the emerging middle class.
d. Merchants who travelled European trade routes.
e. Two of the many Germanic groups who competed for dominance after the fall of Rome.

74. Which of the following events did not take place in the year 1066?

a. The heirless king of the Anglo-Saxons, Edward the Confessor, died.
b. Harold of Wessex was chosen as Edward's successor.
c. William the Conqueror led forces across the English Channel to battle Harold's forces at the Battle of Hastings.
d. The English army mutinied to avoid battle, granting William power without bloodshed.
e. William brought the customs of monarchial feudalism to England.

75. Which of the following statements is not true of the Magna Carta?

a. In 1215, powerful nobles almost overthrew King John, who signed the Magna Carta in order to stay in power.
b. It took away nearly all of the powers of the monarchy.
c. The term means "Great Charter."
d. It held monarchs to the same laws as others.
e. It provided many rights to citizens.

76. A French peasant girl, Joan of Arc, had visions from the saints. What did they tell her to do?

a. Lead French troops to attack the English.
b. Lead troops to retake control of Jerusalem.
c. Become the first female priest in the Catholic Church.
d. Overthrow Charles VII of France.
e. To lead the Children's Crusade.

77. Which of the following is not a cause of the first Crusade?

a. The Turks overtook Jerusalem in 1065.
b. 3,000 Christian pilgrims were massacred in Jerusalem.
c. Turks threatened to invade Constantinople.
d. Pope Urban II argued that defense of Jerusalem was a Christian obligation, sparking a holy war.
e. To distract the public from the abuse of power seen during the Inquisition.

78. Launched in the late 1200s, the Inquisition attempted to

a. Identify heretics and undermine the growing threat of Christian sects.
b. Inspire a holy war against Muslims.
c. Unite the eastern and western branches of the Catholic Church.
d. To resolve the tensions between the church and the kings of European nation-states.
e. Root out abuses of power in the Catholic Church.

79. Which of the following statements does not describe the Great Schism?

a. Several powerful kings began to contest the authority of the Church.
b. King Philip IV of France used his political influence to install a pope whom he could control.
c. The Eastern Orthodox Church and the Roman Catholic Church separated.
d. The pope was moved from Italy to Avignon, France.
e. Different political factions each instated their own popes, with as many as three popes ruling at once.

80. "In 1207, he decided to abandon all of his material possessions and devote himself to serve God. Soon, many followed his path and committed themselves to a life of poverty and service to the poor in an attempt to emulate the life of Jesus."

Who is the person described in this passage?

a. John Wycliffe.
b. Jan Hus.
c. St. Francis of Assisi.
d. Pope Leo III.
e. Martin Luther.

81. "As the Crusades opened up new trade routes to the East, they also forged stronger bonds between Europe and the Byzantine Empire, which had preserved many of the great works of Greek and Roman science. As a result, Europe's interest in philosophy and science was rekindled, and a period of rapid intellectual advancement began."

What is the era described in this passage is known as?

a. The Reformation.
b. Middle Ages.
c. The Renaissance.
d. The Counter Reformation.
e. The Scientific Revolution.

82. Members of this wealthy family were famous for financing many great works by Italian artists in the 15th Century. They were known as patrons.

a. The Medici.
b. The Machiavelli.
c. The Ghiberti.
d. The Brunischelli.
e. The Botticelli.

83. The 15th Century produced many influential artists in Florence, Italy whose work shaped much of what would become recognized as Renaissance art. Which of the following was not an artist from Florence?

a. Filippo Brunelleschi.
b. Masaccio.
c. Lorenzo Ghiberti.
d. Sandro Botticelli.
e. Erasmus.

84. "This school of thought first emerged in the 1300s among Europeans who studied ancient Greek and Roman grammar, history, poetry, and rhetoric. They believed strongly in human dignity, looked for common bonds between different religions and philosophies, and strove for a civilization that would be enriched by learning."

What is the school of thought described in this paragraph?

a. Humanism.
b. Scholasticism.
c. Philosophy.
d. Syncretism.
e. Classicism.

85. Which of the following is not a major work by Michelangelo?

a. Frescoes on the ceiling of the Sistine Chapel.
b. Pieta.
c. David.
d. The Last Judgment.
e. Mona Lisa.

86. Leonardo Da Vinci made important contributions to engineering, architecture, painting, sculpture, and science. Which of the following terms best describes him?

a. Reformist.
b. Renaissance Man.
c. Humanist.
d. Artist.
e. Realist.

87. The country of Flanders produced many masters of the medium of oil painting, known as the Flemish School. Which of the following is not a member of the Flemish school?

a. Jan van Eyck.
b. Hubert van Eyck.
c. Pieter Brueghel.
d. Gerard David.
e. Raphael.

88. Which English humanist authored *Utopia?*

a. Erasmus.
b. William Shakespeare.
c. Albrecht Durer.
d. Thomas More.
e. John Milton.

89. "He became king at the age of three, and as an adult he committed himself to the modernization of his country. He gave himself the title 'czar' (which is the Russian word for 'Caesar': created a modern legal code, forged strong trade alliances, and conquered a vast territory for Russia. Though he saw his country through significant progress, he was also ruthless in persecuting those he saw as political enemies, including his own son."

Who is the Russian king described in this passage?

a. Ivan the Terrible.
b. Michael Romanov.
c. Genghis Khan.
d. Ivan the Great.
e. Ivan I.

90. Which of the following kingdoms was not part of the unification of the Iberian Peninsula now known as Spain?

a. Aragon.
b. Castile.
c. Granada.
d. Kiev.
e. Navarre.

91. Why did Henry VIII's daughter, Mary Tudor, earn the nickname "Bloody Mary"?

a. She violently drove the Moors from her country.
b. She declared war against France.
c. She persecuted members of the Anglican Church.
d. She refused to grant the king a divorce.
e. She persecuted Catholics.

92. To what does the term "indulgence" refer?

a. Priests granting a reduction of punishment for sins.
b. Political pardons offered by kings.
c. Commissions for portraits.
d. Patronizing or financing artists.
e. Excessive imagery in Renaissance art.

93. Which of the following is not a byproduct of the invention of the printing press?

a. A challenge to church authority because people could read the Bible for themselves.
b. An increase in literacy.
c. The Great Schism, a period when the authority of the church was separated between multiple popes.
d. The rapid spread of ideas.
e. The spread of education.

94. Which of the following is not a core belief of Martin Luther?

a. Individuals should read the Bible for themselves.
b. Priests should charge money for the forgiveness of sins.
c. Humans cannot earn salvation by good deeds alone.
d. True faith in God matters above all else.
e. A fee for indulgences was wrong.

95. What is the main reason King Henry VIII started the Anglican Church?

a. He was an advocate of Martin Luther.
b. The pope refused to grant him a divorce.
c. He wished to become pope.
d. He wished to rule over all Catholics.
e. He questioned the divinity of Jesus.

96. "Her strong support of the Anglican Church, her devotion to her role as Queen—to the extent of never marrying—and her generous patronage of popular arts all helped establish her as a popular and beloved Queen. Despite her popularity among her subjects, England was under threat for much of her reign. She uncovered an assassination plot led by her cousin, Mary Queen of Scots, and Phillip II of Spain, which in part brought about war between England and Spain."

Who is the queen described in this passage?

a. Elizabeth I.
b. Anne Boleyn.
c. Mary Tudor.
d. Catherine of Aragon.
e. Isabella.

97. Which of the following reflects a point of disagreement between the theologies of John Calvin and Martin Luther?

a. Jesus' divinity.
b. The trinity of God the Father, God the Son, and God the Holy Spirit.
c. The doctrine of the Eucharist.
d. The reform of the Catholic Church.
e. Justification by faith alone.

98. Which of the following statements is not true of the Counter Reformation?

a. It was founded by Pope Paul III.
b. The pope responded to Protestant criticisms of the Catholic Church.
c. It called for a return to spirituality and ethics among the church leadership.
d. It called for a war against Protestants.
e. It called for assemblies to clarify church doctrine.

99. Which of the following is not true of the Council of Trent?

a. It established the official canon of Biblical books.
b. It ruled that one could only receive forgiveness through priests.
c. It declared that salvation could be gained through good deeds as well as faith.
d. It renounced the doctrine of original sin.
e. It established the methods of penance for one's sins.

100. Who is the Italian writer whose book *The Prince* made his name synonymous with duplicity and dishonesty?

a. Francesco Petrarch.
b. Baldassare Castiglione.
c. Filippo Brunelleschi.
d. Sandro Botticelli.
e. Niccolo Machiavelli.

101. Which of the following cities was known as the "Third Rome"?

a. Kiev.
b. Moscow.
c. London.
d. Paris.
e. Constantinople.

102. Who was not an early explorer of the Americas?

a. Amerigo Vespucci.
b. Ferdinand Magellan.
c. John Cabot.
d. Henry Hudson.
e. Ignatius Loyola.

103. Which of the following statements is not true of the rash of witch hunts that took place in the 14th through 16th centuries in Europe?

a. The witch hunts used the Inquisition's techniques for rooting out heretics.
b. Many hunts followed careful legal codes.
c. Much of the evidence used was based on hearsay.
d. Belief in magic and superstition was commonplace even among educated Europeans.
e. It is estimated that between 40,000 and 100,000 suspected witches were killed during the Early Modern period.

104. Which of the following technological advancements did not lead to increased sea travel?

a. Improvements in mapmaking.
b. Improvements in the compass.
c. The invention of the astrolabe.
d. Improvements in shipbuilding.
e. Development of the steam engine.

105. Which of the following is not a reason why Europeans began colonizing other lands?

a. They wanted to Christianize other peoples they viewed as savages.
b. Drought, famine, and war had destroyed most of Europe.
c. They needed to find additional sources of silver and gold to coin money.
d. They could establish new markets for goods produced in Europe.
e. They could reduce overpopulation in the home country by sending colonists to new regions.

106. Which of the following is not part of triangular trade?

a. Sailing from Europe to Africa.
b. Trading goods for slaves.
c. Selling the slaves to plantation owners in the Americas.
d. Trading American goods in Asia.
e. Selling American goods in Europe.

107. Which American city did the Dutch East India Company purchase in 1626 and name New Amsterdam?

a. Charleston.
b. New York City.
c. New Orleans.
d. Boston.
e. Philadelphia.

108. Why did enmity and hostility grow between Spain and England in the late 1500s?

a. The creation of the Anglican Church angered Catholic Spain.
b. Members of British royalty conspired to assassinate the Spanish king.
c. England had supported Turkish invaders who attempted to attack Spain in the early 1500s.
d. Spain financed pirate attacks on English vessels.
e. Spain supported an anti-English uprising in the Netherlands.

109. In what region did the Thirty Years' War take place?

a. Eastern Europe.
b. The British Isles.
c. Spain.
d. France.
e. Italy.

110. To what does the "long Parliament" refer?

a. A period when King James I clashed with Parliament because they denied his requests to raise taxes.
b. An eleven-year period when King Charles refused to allow Parliament to convene except when absolutely necessary.
c. Queen Elizabeth's reign, because she rarely called the Parliament into session.
d. A period when Parliament opposed English sea trade, which limited competition with other countries pursuing colonization.
e. The period when Parliament attempted to oppose the creation of the Anglican Church.

111. Even though Elizabeth I claimed they were renegades over whom she had no control, what were the seadogs financed by the British to do?

a. Spy on rival governments.
b. Attack the ships of rivals at sea.
c. Smuggle illegal trade items.
d. Assassinate political enemies.
e. Sabotage rival countries' colonies abroad.

112. Which of the following factors did not contribute to Spain's decline as a global power in the 16th Century?

a. England's defeat of the Spanish Armada in 1588.
b. A failed invasion of France.
c. A huge trade deficit.
d. Invasions by Moors who overtook much of the region.
e. The Reconquista, an attempt to drive all non-Catholics out of Spain, which effectively cost Spain all of their talents and innovations.

113. The Cavaliers and Roundheads were warring factions in what event?

a. The English Civil War.
b. The Long Parliament.
c. The Thirty Years War.
d. The Reformation.
e. The Netherlands' rebellion against Spain.

114. What did the Scientific Revolution emphasize?

a. Tradition and authority.
b. Observation and reason.
c. Superstition.
d. Theology.
e. Mythology.

115. Who is the author of *Dialogue Concerning the Two Chief World Systems, Ptolemaic and Copernican* that argued the Earth was not the center of the universe?

a. Copernicus.
b. Galileo Galilei.
c. Johannes Kepler.
d. Rene Descartes.
e. Francis Bacon.

116. This medical scientist was the first to describe how blood cycles throughout the veins and heart.

a. Francis Bacon.
b. Roger Bacon.
c. William Harvey.
d. Ambroise Paré.
e. Andreas Vesalius.

117. Which of the following does not reflect a basic belief of the Puritans?

a. They believed the Anglican Church had lost touch with the best aspects of the Catholic tradition.
b. They believed the elect are predestined to salvation.
c. Their theology was closer to Calvinism than to Anglicanism.
d. They wanted to purify the Anglican Church and remove all remnants of Catholicism.
e. They believed individuals should have a personal religious experience.

118. "The first English settlement in North America, this town was primarily established as an economic venture. The colonists who arrived in the region in 1607 had been sent there for financial purposes, not necessarily for the religious freedoms that motivated later settlements. Several years passed before it turned its first profit with a tobacco crop in 1614, and the years between its settlement and its first economic successes were a period of lawlessness and starvation for many of the settlers."

What is the town described in this passage?

a. Plymouth.
b. Jamestown.
c. Charleston.
d. St. Augustine.
e. Salem.

119. Which of the following statements is not true of daily life for the average European in the 1500s?

a. Life was not significantly different from the medieval era.
b. The majority of people worked in agriculture.
c. Life expectancy was short.
d. Most people were literate, due to well-financed public education programs.
e. The Commercial Revolution and the colonization of new lands made new opportunities possible for the first time.

120. Which of the following statements does not describe the average European diet BEFORE the expansion of trade routes?

a. Europeans ate for survival, not enjoyment.
b. They had an abundance of preservatives such as salt that could make food last longer.
c. Grain-based foods such as porridge and bread were staple meals.
d. Spices were unavailable.
e. Luxury items such as tea, sugar, and coffee had not yet been introduced.

Answer Key and Explanations

1. C: Though Egypt had a well-known pictographic writing system called hieroglyphs, other cultures used different forms of writing. For example, cuneiform is a language that does not use pictographs. The remaining choices played an essential role in all early civilizations.

2. A: Roman civilization developed on the Tiber River, but it is not considered one of the earliest civilizations. Major civilizations developed along the other rivers listed: Chinese civilization developed in the Yangtze and Huang River valleys; Mesopotamian civilization emerged between the Tigris and Euphrates; and Egyptian culture developed in the Nile River valley.

3. C: This passage contains two clues to the answer: one the river flows north and two the river lies to the south of the Mediterranean Sea. The Nile is the only river listed that flows south-to-north and lies to the south of the Mediterranean, making Choice C the best choice. These geographical clues can be used to exclude the other choices: the Tiber is incorrect because it lies to the north of the Mediterranean Sea. The other choices are incorrect because these rivers lie east or southeast of the sea.

4. C: Hatshepsut was an Egyptian Pharaoh whose name means "foremost of noble ladies." Sargon, Hammurabi, Nebuchadnezzar, and Amenhotep IV were men.

5. E: This passage details the political hierarchy of the Sumerian government. Little mention is made of agricultural surplus, population centers, or technology. Choice C is incorrect because the passage primarily focuses on the structure of Sumerian government.

6. B: The Mesopotamian civilization developed in the Tigris and Euphrates River Valley, an area now controlled by Iraq. None of the other answers encompass this region.

7. A: The word "Satrap" is associated with Persian governors, not Akkadians, Babylonians, or Egyptians.

8. B: Of the cultures listed, only the Hebrews worshipped one God. Egyptians, Sumerians, Babylonians, and Hittites all practiced polytheistic religions that worshipped a host of deities.

9. B: Enkidu is a character in the *Epic of Gilgamesh.* Ahura Mazda is a deity in the Zoroastrian religion. Yahweh is the God of the Hebrew people. Thoth is one of the many Egyptian deities. Zoroaster is the prophet of the Zoroastrian religion.

10. B: Abraham is considered the founder of the Israelite tradition. Zoroaster is not directly associated with the Israelite tradition. Aeneas is a character from Greek legends, sometimes associated with the founding of Rome. Though Daniel and Jesus shaped the history of the Israelite people and religion, neither is considered the founder.

11. E: Ziggurats are tall stair-stepped towers built by Mesopotamians. The remaining choices are true: The Phoenicians developed purple dyes associated with royalty, sailing technology used all over the ancient world, an alphabet which formed the foundation of many writing systems still in use, and influential metalworking practices.

12. D: Around 600 BC, the Lydians of Asia Minor were one of the first to coin metal currency.

13. C: is the best choice because Athenian culture developed more than a thousand years later than Minoan. The remaining choices all reflect true statements, so none is the best choice for the question. The legendary King Minos is the namesake for the island. Knossos was the center of Minoan culture and its capital was on the island of Crete. The capital was a mazelike structure from which we derive the term "labyrinth." Many frescoes, or wall paintings, have been uncovered and reconstructed provide scholars a great source of information about Minoan culture.

14. A: The word "democracy" comes from two Greek root words: *demos* "people" and *kratia* "rule."

15. A: Members of the slave class of ancient Sparta were called helots. Hoplites, refers to a type of foot soldier. The ephorate was a governing body in Sparta. Metics is a term that refers to a class of people living in Athens who were not Athenian citizens by birth and who could not own land or run for political office. Archon refers to a governing body in Athens that assumed the duties of the former kings.

16. A: Draco was an Athenian who sentenced offenders to death for minor infractions. The word "Draconian" is still used today to refer to unusually harsh punishments. Solon is the legendary reformer of the Athenian legal system. Alcibiades is an Athenian famous for leading the navy in a disastrous campaign in Sicily. Pericles is the Athenian leader who incurred the resentment of other city-states in ancient Greece because of the amount of power he amassed. Aristophanes is considered the greatest author of comedies of the classical period.

17. C: The historical record indicates the Greeks were outnumbered by the Persians many times over. Persian forces did invade the Greek mainland in retaliation for Athens' involvement in an uprising against Persian Satraps in Asia Minor. Greek soldiers did repel the Persian army at the Battle of Marathon. Persian forces did penetrate Greek defenses to sack Athens. Athens and Sparta did align themselves against Persia in their defense of the Greek mainland.

18. D: The *Iliad* and *Odyssey* were most likely composed in the 8th Century, B.C., not during the golden age of Pericles, which lasted from the end of the Persian Wars in 448 B.C. to the beginning of the Peloponnesian Wars in 404 B.C. Pericles' oversight of Athens coincides directly with the life of Socrates, the great philosopher. The Acropolis was restored during Pericles' time. The art form of the tragedy flourished while Pericles was in power. The famous histories of Herodotus and Thucydides were written during Pericles' time.

19. D: Athens did not invade Sparta. Athens' power did create resentment among other Greek city-states. Athens' monopoly on trade accounts for a significant cause of the war. Sparta did establish an alliance to counteract the power of Athens. The Spartans did invade Attica, an area near Athens.

20. B: The *Odyssey* focuses on Odysseus, but he is only one of many characters depicted in the *Iliad.* Both epics deal with the Trojan War or its aftermath. Both works are attributed to Homer, even if some scholars have reason to doubt the attribution. The works appear to be written in the 8th Century, B.C. Both poems extend from an oral tradition.

21. C: Athena was the goddess of war, wisdom, and the arts. Aphrodite was the goddess of love. Hera was the goddess of marriage. Demeter was an Earth goddess, whose name comes from a combination of the words "Earth" and "mother." Artemis was often depicted as the goddess of the hunt.

22. B: The word derives from the Greek word for wisdom, which is also the root of "philosophy" and "sophisticated." Philosophers is not as accurate as sophists. Rhetoricians and orators refer to public speakers, not private tutors. Although the sophists vetted their students for a life in politics, politicians were primarily educators.

23. C: Athenian women were not allowed to vote. The other choices are all true of Athenian women. Many families practiced infanticide, killing female infants. Women were expected to govern the household. The public domain was not considered the proper place for a woman. Women were not allowed to own or inherit any property.

24. B: Phillip of Macedon defeated Greek troops in the Battle of Chaeronea in 338 B.C. The remaining choices are incorrect.

25. E: Choices A, B, and C are implausible or historically inaccurate. Choice D is incorrect because Rome did not begin to expand its empire during these decades.

26. C: Each of these statements is historically true except Choice C. Alexander did not successfully conquer all of India because his troops, weary from years of military campaigns, mutinied. Alexander agreed to return home and conquered many tribes along the western border of the country, but he did not enter the mainland as he intended.

27. D: Alexander's son did not bring peace to the region; he was executed after taking power over the empire. Each of the remaining choices is true statements about the period after Alexander's death.

28. B: The Greeks believed excess brought about negative consequences, while moderation did not. The remaining choices reflect other cultures' values, some of which are present in Greek culture; however, the theme of moderation dominates Greek writing and art.

29. C: The belief that humanity has fallen from grace is more in keeping with Christian beliefs. Furthermore, the faces of Greek statues rarely express humility. The expressionless faces of Greek statuary capture the belief that strong emotion should not be expressed in public. Each of the remaining statements is a valid interpretation. The symmetry and precision of Greek architecture was achieved through the application of geometrical and mathematical principles. The Greeks placed a high value on athletic skill as evidenced in the popularity of the Olympic Games. Much Greek art was functional. Simplicity was valued above excess and this value is reflected in the art.

30. B: The majority of our knowledge of Socrates' philosophy comes from the writing of Plato, and to a lesser extent, the writing of his contemporary, Xenophon. Socrates never wrote anything down. In one of Plato's dialogs, he speaks out against the written word, arguing that it makes the memory weaker if people become too reliant on it. The comedian Aristophanes did depict Socrates in his play *The Clouds,* however, the comedic work only parodies and doesn't explore in any depth. Many works about Socrates were written during his lifetime and shortly thereafter.

31. A: The most significant clue is the name Pyrrho, who founded the school of skepticism. Epicureanism held that people should seek pleasure and minimize pain to get the most out of life. The cynics promoted a life without concern for social status, physical pleasure, or wealth. The stoics placed the pursuit of wisdom above all other goals. Dualism is a generic term for a philosophy that divides the world into two parts: mind / body, spiritual / material, etc.

32. E: Democritus was a Greek philosopher whose argument that the world is composed of tiny, indivisible atoms has been confirmed by science. The atomic theory is primarily attributed to Democritus and his mentor Leucippus.

33. B: Socrates is not considered the first to argue in favor of the atomic theory. The remaining choices are true statements about the contributions of Greek thinkers to science.

34. A: The three works are the only extant trilogy, though most works of Greek drama were composed as trilogies. The three plays written about Oedipus were written by Sophocles and were not technically a trilogy. Sophocles' plays were composed and performed at different times while Aeschylus' works were composed to be performed together. The remaining choices are not trilogies.

35. A: Herodotus' *Histories* tells the story of the Persian invasion of Greece. It covers many historical topics, but its central focus is the Persian Wars. Choice B is associated with the Trojan War, which is not the main subject of Herodotus' work. Choice C is covered by Thucydides in *The History of the Peloponnesian Wars*. Choice D, the legend of King Oedipus, was depicted in Sophocles' dramatic works. Choice E reflects the content of many plays and epics, but not the central focus of Herodotus' *Histories.*

36. E: Plato is the philosopher described in the passage. Aristotle famously disagreed with the theory of forms, preferring to focus on the natural world itself instead of the ideal world of forms that Plato described. Thales is primarily remembered for his contributions to geometry and his belief that water is the principle element from which all matter extends. Anaxagoras is best remembered for his mathematical arguments and his theory that material substances are the result of an immaterial force or spirit that he called "nous," which translates as "mind." Parmenides is remembered for his use of logical deduction to determine the fundamental principles of nature.

37. B: The harsh educational techniques were practiced in Sparta, not Athens. The remaining choices are all reflections of Athenian educational practice.

38. B: The Etruscans were from a kingdom to the north that seized control of Rome from the Latins in the mid-600s BC. They began urbanizing the settlement, improving roads, adding drainage systems, etc. They were driven out of the region in 509 BC during an uprising of the Latins.

39. C: The city of Rome was founded around 753 B.C. The remaining statements are true of the Latins.

40. A: This passage describes the Senate, A. The Magistrates were composed of several groups, each with different responsibilities. The remaining choices were all part of the Magistrates. Praetors were responsible for overseeing the legal system and the army. The Censors enforced the moral code of the Romans. The Consuls were two chief executives who made important decisions for the Republic. Their ability to veto one another is one of the earliest examples of a system of checks and balances.

41. D: The effects of the Punic Wars include the development of a strong Roman naval force, the destruction of Carthage, the increased influence of Rome in the region, and the loss of Macedonian influence.

42. D: The Conflict of the Orders refers to a disagreement between Roman commoners, the Plebeians and the wealthy aristocracy, the Patricians. Until the 4th Century B.C., Patricians had complete control of the Roman Senate and held great political power in spite of representing only a small percentage of the population. The Patricians routinely abused their power, for example, selling wealthy Plebeians into slavery if they failed to repay debts. Plebeians, wealthy landowners in particular, undertook a variety of largely peaceful protests and were awarded political representation in 287 B.C. These events led to the composition of the "Twelve Tables," legal documents, which became the foundation of Roman law.

43. C: The remaining events occurred throughout the Punic Wars, but none identifies the primary event that sparked the wars. A: triggered the Second Punic War in 218 B.C. Choice B took place in 146 B.C. at the end of the Punic Wars. Choice D happened after the Second Punic War in 197 B.C. Choice E occurred in 204 B.C., during the Second Punic War.

44. B: Caesar's political rivals and former allies assassinated him because they feared his power. Choice A is true of Tiberius. Choice C describes an infamous political appointment made by Caligula. Choice D recounts one of Caesar's famous military actions, but was not the principle reason for his assassination. Choice E is true of Marc Antony, who attacked Augustus in 31 B.C., after Caesar's death.

45. E: Marcus Aurelius, is the only emperor among those listed who was not a member of the Julio-Claudian line. The first emperor from this family lineage was Augustus. He was followed by Tiberius, Caligula and Claudius. The lineage ended in 68 A.D. with the suicide of Nero.

46. A: Choice B refers to several influential tribunes and consuls from the 1st and 2nd Centuries B.C. Choice C is the three emperors who took power and were assassinated in the year following Nero's suicide. Choice D refers to the five claimants to the throne in the year 193 A.D. Choice E is the five emperors from the Julio-Claudian line.

47. C: The passage describes the 200-year period known as *Pax Romana.* Choice A is incorrect because the Julio-Claudian line held power in Rome for less than a century. Choice B refers to a succession of emperors that lasted less than one hundred years. The emperors in Choice D only ruled from 69 A.D. to 96 A.D. (E) is two tribunes who attempted to lead reforms in the 2nd Century B.C.

48. C: The Forum, the Pantheon, the Coliseum and the House of the Vestal Virgins are all major structures in the city of Rome. Hadrian's Wall is in England.

49. C: Spartacus was the leader of a slave rebellion.

50. D: Homer is the ancient Greek author of the *Iliad* and the *Odyssey*. Horace was a Roman poet, the source of many popular Latin phrases, such as *carpe diem*, "seize the day." His works include *Odes*, *Satires*, and *Ars Poetica.* Livy was a famous Roman historian whose only surviving work is the *History of Rome.* Plutarch wrote many works. One of his best known works is a collection of biographies, referred to as *Lives*, which recount the lives of great Greek figures and compare them to great Romans. Each contains a philosophical reflection on the lessons to be learned from each figure's accomplishments and character. Virgil is best known for his epic, the *Aeneid*, which recounts the mythical history of Rome and connects the country's origins to the great Greeks who fought in the Trojan War.

51. C: The *Metamorphoses* collects many Roman and Greek myths. The book was written in 8 A.D. and was the primary source for understanding Greek mythology throughout the medieval period. Ovid had a huge impact on Shakespeare.

52. C: Starting with Edward Gibbon's tome, *The Decline and Fall of the Roman Empire*, many historians attributed the gradual decline of power in Rome to moral corruption. These historians often cite the bloody gladiator battles and executions as examples of the deterioration of Roman morals.

53. B: Paul of Tarsus played one of the most significant roles in the development of the early Christian Church.

54. A: As part of a larger effort to combat supporters of pagan religions in Rome, Theodosius made Christianity the official religion of the Roman Empire in 391 A.D.

55. E: The Etruscans invaded Rome much earlier in its history and had no part in the Germanic invasions of the 5th through 7th Centuries A.D. The Goths, the Ostrogoths and the Visigoths sacked Rome in 410 A.D. The Vandals were the second group to plunder Rome in 455 A.D. The term "vandalism" comes from the destruction this group caused and from their unrestrained looting of Rome's wealth and art. The Huns attacked many Roman territories in the middle of the 5th Century.

56. C: It is the only one that does NOT contribute to the split between the eastern and western Empires. The Crusades did not begin until the 11th Century A.D. Emperor Diocletian attempted to make the empire easier to rule by dividing it into two separate centers of control, which established a precedent for separating the eastern empire from the western. Though emperors after Diocletian did succeed in reuniting the empire, corruption threatened to tear the kingdom apart again. Over time, Constantinople, the seat of power in the eastern Empire, amassed more power and influence. The gap between the rich and poor widened considerably in the West, leading to a loss of faith in the government and a gradual decline in strength. Constantinople and the eastern empire continued to thrive.

57. A: Most of the conquered peoples were not granted Roman citizenship. Each conquered state was allowed some degree of cultural autonomy. Subjects were expected to follow the laws of Rome, pay taxes, and hand over land and supplies to the Roman government.

58. A: The Justinian Code was a collection of Roman laws and legal opinions. In the 6th Century A.D., Justinian assembled a collection of jurists to bring together the most important works of Roman law including public laws and legal opinions.

59. B: The iconoclasts opposed the use of religious images, or icons, in worship. Choice E does reflect part of the argument made by proponents of icons, namely that it helped to spread Christianity to the illiterate masses. By the 7th Century A.D., images of Jesus and the saints gained popularity for use in worship. Many Christians believed that the worship of images was a false form of religion. In the 8th Century, Emperor Leo III of Byzantium and Pope Adrian I outlawed the worship of icons. This decision eventually led to the split between the Roman Catholic and Eastern Orthodox Churches.

60. E: The first obligation of Islam, the profession of faith, is "shahadah." The second requirement, five daily prayers, is "salat." Contributing to the poor and needy is the third obligation, "zakat." A pilgrimage to the city of Mecca "hajj," is the fifth requirement. Not listed is the fourth pillar, "sawm," fasting during the day for one month of the year.

61. B: Imam refers to leaders of the Shiite sect. Sultan refers to a Turkish Muslim government leader. Sheik refers to an elder or leader in an Arabic tribe. Vizier was a member of the Turkish Islamic government.

62. D: Each answer describes a significant contribution Arabic thinkers made to the sciences except D, the abacus, which predates Arabic culture.

63. D: Each answers presents one of the main reasons Europe entered a period of fragmentation, referred to as the "Dark Ages," except Choice D. There was no global collapse of civilization during this time; sciences and arts continued to flourish in many other cultures.

64. A: The person described in this passage is Charlemagne, King of the Franks (742-814). Pope Leo III was a contemporary and ally of Charlemagne. Charles Martel was best known for halting Muslim expansion by defeating invading armies at the Battle of Tours in 732. Clovis I and Pepin II were both responsible for bringing unity to the Frankish tribes.

65. C: Fief refers to the section of land a lord might grant. Homage refers to the oath of loyalty the recipient of the land would make to the lord. Primogeniture refers to the system of inheritance that granted the son of a lord complete ownership and control of his landholdings. Vassal is the person who would receive land from the lord.

66. C: Each statement accurately describes the system of manorialism except Choice C. Serfs could not, as a rule, become nobles by working hard.

67. D: Each statement describes the hierarchy of the Catholic Church except Choice D. The curia was a group of archbishops who elected new popes, but the ultimate authority was the pope.

68. B: Heretic is a term used to describe one who has been excommunicated. Interdict refers to the church's authority to keep entire regions from receiving the sacraments. Canon law refers to the code of law that governed the church. Indulgences refer to the widely criticized practice of charging fees for the forgiveness of sins.

69. E: The practice of chivalry refers to a code of conduct among knights. Serfs were peasants who worked the land and gave the crops to the lord, keeping enough for their own sustenance. Archbishops were members of the Roman Catholic church hierarchy. Troubadours were travelling musicians whose songs about chivalry kept the code alive in the popular imagination. Vassals were nobles who received land from lords in compensation for their loyalty and protection.

70. A: Choice B refers to Geoffrey Chaucer. Choice C refers to Dante Alighieri. Choice D refers to St. Francis of Assisi. Choice E refers to the work of St. Augustine.

71. D: Charters refer to land grants that allowed citizens of towns certain rights. Fief refers to a land granted by a lord to a vassal, a lower noble, in exchange for loyalty and protection. Manor refers to a lord's landholdings. Banks refers to moneychangers.

72. B: The Black Death refers to the plague that swept through 14th century Europe. Bubonic plague, brought in by rats on shipping vessels, is believed to have been the primary cause, though some question this theory.

73. E: The Angles and Saxons were two of the Germanic groups who competed for power after the fall of Rome. It is from them that the term Anglo-Saxons originated.

74. D: Each of the answers describes a key event of the year 1066 except Choice D. The English army did not avoid battle. The Battle of Hastings was a bloody conflict that resulted in the devastation of the English army. William the Conqueror took control of England and brought Norman customs and government, which shaped the culture of England.

75. B: Each of the answers is true except Choice B. The Magna Carta did not take the powers of the monarchy away. It did, however, hold the monarchy to the same rule of law as commoners.

76. A: Joan of Arc was a French peasant who had visions of saints telling her to lead the French army in an attack against the English. She eventually led the French to a victorious battle against the English in 1429. Several years later she was brought before the Inquisition by political enemies, found guilty of heresy, and sentenced to death.

77. E: Each of the choices is true except Choice E. The Crusades occurred before the Inquisition.

78. A: None of the other answers applies to the Inquisition. These historical events began in 1224 when Pope Gregory IX began investigating, torturing and executing suspected heretics. These measures were initially undertaken to combat the growing threat of Christian sects that sought to undermine the authority of the Catholic Church.

79. C: Each of the answers is true of the Great Schism except Choice C. The Catholic Church split into eastern and western factions in 1054. The Great Schism refers to the splintering of the Catholic Church's power as the kings of several different regions attempted to install their own popes.

80. C: St. Francis of Assisi, is the best answer. John Wycliffe and Jan Hus were early reformers of the Catholic Church who believed that individuals should be educated and that bishops and clergy held too much power. Pope Leo III was in power during the reign of Charlemagne. Martin Luther was a church reformer who eventually split with the Catholic Church, sparking the Protestant Reformation.

81. C: The Reformation refers to a time when attempts to reform the Catholic Church led to a split between Catholic and Protestant groups. The Middle Ages refers to the period between the fall of the Roman Empire and the beginning of the Renaissance, an era sometimes referred to as the "Dark Ages." The Counter Reformation was a period when the pope attempted to address the criticisms of Protestant reformers and reform the Catholic Church. The Scientific Revolution refers to a period when traditional interpretations of the natural world were replaced with interpretations based on the scientific method of careful observation.

82. A: The Medici were a powerful, wealthy family, famous for their financial contributions to artists in Florence.

83. E: Brunelleschi was an architect whose most famous construction is the Duomo in Florence. Masaccio was a painter whose frescoes demonstrate an early attempt to develop perspective that would later give Renaissance paintings their striking realism. Lorenzo Ghiberti was a sculptor noted for his "Gates of Paradise," the doors of the cathedral in Florence, adorned with sculptures depicting biblical scenes. Botticelli was a noted painter whose works include *Primavera* and *Birth of Venus.*

84. A: Scholasticism refers to the work of St. Thomas Aquinas who attempted to use formal logic to address issues of divinity and Christian faith. Philosophy is a very broad term encompassing humanism and many other intellectual movements. Syncretism refers to the practice of reconciling contradictory beliefs between religions. Classicism refers to students of Ancient Greek and Roman culture. Though the humanists were students of the classics, their work reflects a philosophy different from strict classicism.

85. E: The *Mona Lisa,* is the only painting not created by Michelangelo. The artist was Leonardo Da Vinci.

86. B: Though Choices (C), (D), and (E) apply to Da Vinci, the question describes him as a man with great learning and skills in a variety of fields, which is the definition of a Renaissance Man.

87. E: Raphael, is the only artist not a member of the Flemish school. Jan and Hubert van Eyck were brothers who perfected of the technique of oil painting. Brueghel often depicted images of peasants in order to criticize the injustices he witnessed. Gerard David was renowned for the use of colors in his illustrated manuscripts and miniatures.

88. D: Thomas More, was the author of *Utopia* that described an ideal society with no private property and equality for all.

89. A: Ivan the Terrible, also known as Ivan IV, is the Russian king described. Michael Romanov would come to power in Russia after Ivan's reign. Genghis Khan conquered Russia in the 13th Century before Ivan's reign. Ivan the Terrible was a member of the Rurik lineage, which included his father, Ivan the Great, and the first of the Ivans to rule Russia, Ivan I.

90. D: Kiev, is part of Russia. The other choices were separate Kingdoms in the Iberian Peninsula — the area known as Spain — until Ferdinand and Isabella began consolidating the regions in the late 15th Century.

91. C: A devout Catholic, Mary Tudor was known as "Bloody Mary" for her violent opposition to members of the Anglican Church, which her father, Henry VIII, created. She once burned 300 religious dissidents at the stake.

92. A: The term "indulgence" refers to the Catholic practice of priests reducing the punishment for a sin. In the 16th Century when priests began charging a fee for indulgences, Martin Luther vehemently opposed abuses related to indulgences.

93. C: Each shows a significant consequence of the printing press except Choice C. The Great Schism took place in the 14th and 15th Centuries when kings and other political influences began to erode the authority of the Catholic Church.

94. B: Each of the other statements reflects one of Martin Luther's core beliefs.

95. B: Choice B accounts for Henry VIII's decision to create the Anglican Church. He wanted a male heir, but his marriage to Catherine of Aragon gave him only daughters. When he requested a divorce, Pope Clement VII denied him. In response, he joined the Protestant movement and established the Anglican Church.

96. A: The queen described is Elizabeth I. Anne Boleyn was Henry VIII's second wife, stepmother to Elizabeth I. Mary Tudor was Elizabeth's sister, known as "Bloody Mary." Catherine of Aragon was Henry VIII's first wife, Elizabeth's mother. Isabella was the Queen of Spain.

97. C: The doctrine of the Eucharist. Martin Luther believed that Christ was physically present "in, around, and under" the elements, while John Calvin believed that Christ was not physically present (yet still spiritually present) in the Eucharist. Neither opposed the remaining choices: Jesus's divinity, the Trinity, the need for reform in the Catholic Church, or the doctrine of justification by faith alone.

98. D: The Counter Reformation was a 16th Century movement that wanted to reform the Catholic Church without losing its traditions. It began roughly with the Council of Trent (1545-1643) and ended with the Thirty Years War (1648).

99. D: The Council of Trent met to determine what aspects of Protestant doctrine it considered heretical and to define the Church's position on key issues of the Catholic faith.

100. E: Machiavelli's book *The Prince* promoted a shrewd approach to politics, aimed at maintaining power. Petrarch was a humanist poet, famous for his sonnets. Castiglione wrote a novel disguised as fiction that revealed the lives of government officials and royalty. Brunelleschi was an architect famous for the Duomo. Botticelli was an influential painter from Florence, Italy.

101. B: Moscow took the nickname the "Third Rome," after the fall of Constantinople because it became the center of the Orthodox Church. Since Rome was the first center of the Catholic Church and Constantinople was the second, Moscow attempted to align itself with these great cities.

102. E: Ignatius Loyola founded an order of priests called the Society of Jesus, or Jesuits. Amerigo Vespucci was immortalized when German mapmakers named the new world after him. Magellan was a Portuguese explorer who led the first expedition to travel around the world. John Cabot claimed Newfoundland, Nova Scotia, and areas of New England for England. Henry Hudson explored much of what is now the northeastern United States.

103. B: The witch hunts reflect a time when belief in magic and superstition was widespread. Many historians view them as a reaction to the social and economic changes of the Early Modern period.

104. E: The steam engine was not invented until the 19th Century. The other choices describe a technological innovation that helped improve navigation and shipbuilding technology during the Early Modern period.

105. B: While much drought, famine, and war took place in Europe, none of these events completely destroyed the region. Many people remained in Europe despite expansion abroad.

106. D: Triangular trade refers to the process by which Europeans exchanged goods and slaves with the Americas.

107. B: The Dutch East India Company named the region after the city of Amsterdam. The city was renamed after the British took control of the region in 1664.

108. B: Members of Spanish and British royalty conspired to assassinate Elizabeth I, Queen of England. (C) refers to attacks against the region of Spain in the 700s. (D) is an incorrect statement: England financed the seadogs, pirates who attacked Spanish vessels. (E) is an incorrect statement: the uprising in the Netherlands was against Spain.

109. A: The Thirty Years' War began when the Holy Roman Emperor began to drive Protestants from Bohemia and Austria in 1618. Protestants responded by rebelling, and though they were quickly suppressed, many other rebellions began. They sparked a land-grab in the region, which was finally settled in 1648 with the Treaty of Westphalia, creating several new nations in Eastern Europe.

110. B: The Long Parliament refers to the reign of Charles I whose attempts to raise taxes were repeatedly thwarted by Parliament. In response, Charles refused to allow Parliament to convene for eleven years and attempted to rule England as an absolute monarchy. In 1640, when Charles convened Parliament to help settle a Scottish uprising, Parliament passed laws limiting his power to convene and disband Parliament.

111. B: Though Elizabeth publicly disavowed the group of pirates known as the seadogs, claiming she had no influence or control over their actions, she privately funded their raids on rival countries' sea vessels.

112. D: The Moors invaded Spain in the 700s. Although Spain's decline in power began to accelerate after the defeat of the Spanish Armada, many causes led up to the decline.

113. A: After the period known as the Long Parliament when King Charles I refused to convene Parliament, members of the government attempted to take control of the army. In response, Charles had several leaders of the House of Commons arrested. Soon after, fighting broke out between factions loyal to Charles, known as the Cavaliers, and supporters of Parliament, called the Roundheads.

114. B: The Scientific Revolution emphasized careful observation of the natural world and applied reason to make and test generalizations about how it operated. The Scientific Revolution saw its zenith in the wide-ranging discoveries of Sir Isaac Newton (1642-1727).

115. B: The *Dialogue Concerning the Two Chief World Systems* was written in 1632 by Galileo Galilei. Two characters debate the merits and flaws of the Ptolemaic model, the Earth was the center of the heavens, and the Copernican model, the Earth was not the center of the universe. The Inquisition forced Galileo to publicly retract his support for the Copernican model.

116. C: Francis Bacon was an English philosopher who promoted the scientific method. Roger Bacon was a monk who argued in favor of scientific experimentation to better understand the physical world. Ambroise Paré is considered the father of modern surgery. Andreas Vesalius made an important impact on the study of anatomy.

117. A: The Puritans believed the Anglican Church needed to be purified (hence the name "Puritans") of all remnants of Catholicism.

118. B: The town described is B, Jamestown. Plymouth was founded by Puritan settlers in pursuit of religious freedom. Charleston was also known for its religious tolerance. St. Augustine was founded in 1565 by Spanish settlers and is the oldest continuously inhabited city in the US. Salem was an important seaport.

119. D: Despite the growing amount of literacy in the 1500s, due principally to the invention of the printing press and the availability of texts, the majority of Europeans remained illiterate.

120. B: Salt and other preservatives were known in Europe long before major trade expansions, but they were costly and not abundant for most people; therefore, the claim of an 'abundance of preservatives' is inaccurate.

How to Overcome Test Anxiety

Just the thought of taking a test is enough to make most people a little nervous. A test is an important event that can have a long-term impact on your future, so it's important to take it seriously and it's natural to feel anxious about performing well. But just because anxiety is normal, that doesn't mean that it's helpful in test taking, or that you should simply accept it as part of your life. Anxiety can have a variety of effects. These effects can be mild, like making you feel slightly nervous, or severe, like blocking your ability to focus or remember even a simple detail.

If you experience test anxiety—whether severe or mild—it's important to know how to beat it. To discover this, first you need to understand what causes test anxiety.

Causes of Test Anxiety

While we often think of anxiety as an uncontrollable emotional state, it can actually be caused by simple, practical things. One of the most common causes of test anxiety is that a person does not feel adequately prepared for their test. This feeling can be the result of many different issues such as poor study habits or lack of organization, but the most common culprit is time management. Starting to study too late, failing to organize your study time to cover all of the material, or being distracted while you study will mean that you're not well prepared for the test. This may lead to cramming the night before, which will cause you to be physically and mentally exhausted for the test. Poor time management also contributes to feelings of stress, fear, and hopelessness as you realize you are not well prepared but don't know what to do about it.

Other times, test anxiety is not related to your preparation for the test but comes from unresolved fear. This may be a past failure on a test, or poor performance on tests in general. It may come from comparing yourself to others who seem to be performing better or from the stress of living up to expectations. Anxiety may be driven by fears of the future—how failure on this test would affect your educational and career goals. These fears are often completely irrational, but they can still negatively impact your test performance.

Elements of Test Anxiety

As mentioned earlier, test anxiety is considered to be an emotional state, but it has physical and mental components as well. Sometimes you may not even realize that you are suffering from test anxiety until you notice the physical symptoms. These can include trembling hands, rapid heartbeat, sweating, nausea, and tense muscles. Extreme anxiety may lead to fainting or vomiting. Obviously, any of these symptoms can have a negative impact on testing. It is important to recognize them as soon as they begin to occur so that you can address the problem before it damages your performance.

The mental components of test anxiety include trouble focusing and inability to remember learned information. During a test, your mind is on high alert, which can help you recall information and stay focused for an extended period of time. However, anxiety interferes with your mind's natural processes, causing you to blank out, even on the questions you know well. The strain of testing during anxiety makes it difficult to stay focused, especially on a test that may take several hours. Extreme anxiety can take a huge mental toll, making it difficult not only to recall test information but even to understand the test questions or pull your thoughts together.

Effects of Test Anxiety

Test anxiety is like a disease—if left untreated, it will get progressively worse. Anxiety leads to poor performance, and this reinforces the feelings of fear and failure, which in turn lead to poor performances on subsequent tests. It can grow from a mild nervousness to a crippling condition. If allowed to progress, test anxiety can have a big impact on your schooling, and consequently on your future.

Test anxiety can spread to other parts of your life. Anxiety on tests can become anxiety in any stressful situation, and blanking on a test can turn into panicking in a job situation. But fortunately, you don't have to let anxiety rule your testing and determine your grades. There are a number of relatively simple steps you can take to move past anxiety and function normally on a test and in the rest of life.

Physical Steps for Beating Test Anxiety

While test anxiety is a serious problem, the good news is that it can be overcome. It doesn't have to control your ability to think and remember information. While it may take time, you can begin taking steps today to beat anxiety.

Just as your first hint that you may be struggling with anxiety comes from the physical symptoms, the first step to treating it is also physical. Rest is crucial for having a clear, strong mind. If you are tired, it is much easier to give in to anxiety. But if you establish good sleep habits, your body and mind will be ready to perform optimally, without the strain of exhaustion. Additionally, sleeping well helps you to retain information better, so you're more likely to recall the answers when you see the test questions.

Getting good sleep means more than going to bed on time. It's important to allow your brain time to relax. Take study breaks from time to time so it doesn't get overworked, and don't study right before bed. Take time to rest your mind before trying to rest your body, or you may find it difficult to fall asleep.

Along with sleep, other aspects of physical health are important in preparing for a test. Good nutrition is vital for good brain function. Sugary foods and drinks may give a burst of energy but this burst is followed by a crash, both physically and emotionally. Instead, fuel your body with protein and vitamin-rich foods.

Also, drink plenty of water. Dehydration can lead to headaches and exhaustion, especially if your brain is already under stress from the rigors of the test. Particularly if your test is a long one, drink water during the breaks. And if possible, take an energy-boosting snack to eat between sections.

Along with sleep and diet, a third important part of physical health is exercise. Maintaining a steady workout schedule is helpful, but even taking 5-minute study breaks to walk can help get your blood pumping faster and clear your head. Exercise also releases endorphins, which contribute to a positive feeling and can help combat test anxiety.

When you nurture your physical health, you are also contributing to your mental health. If your body is healthy, your mind is much more likely to be healthy as well. So take time to rest, nourish your body with healthy food and water, and get moving as much as possible. Taking these physical steps will make you stronger and more able to take the mental steps necessary to overcome test anxiety.

Mental Steps for Beating Test Anxiety

Working on the mental side of test anxiety can be more challenging, but as with the physical side, there are clear steps you can take to overcome it. As mentioned earlier, test anxiety often stems from lack of preparation, so the obvious solution is to prepare for the test. Effective studying may be the most important weapon you have for beating test anxiety, but you can and should employ several other mental tools to combat fear.

First, boost your confidence by reminding yourself of past success—tests or projects that you aced. If you're putting as much effort into preparing for this test as you did for those, there's no reason you should expect to fail here. Work hard to prepare; then trust your preparation.

Second, surround yourself with encouraging people. It can be helpful to find a study group, but be sure that the people you're around will encourage a positive attitude. If you spend time with others who are anxious or cynical, this will only contribute to your own anxiety. Look for others who are motivated to study hard from a desire to succeed, not from a fear of failure.

Third, reward yourself. A test is physically and mentally tiring, even without anxiety, and it can be helpful to have something to look forward to. Plan an activity following the test, regardless of the outcome, such as going to a movie or getting ice cream.

When you are taking the test, if you find yourself beginning to feel anxious, remind yourself that you know the material. Visualize successfully completing the test. Then take a few deep, relaxing breaths and return to it. Work through the questions carefully but with confidence, knowing that you are capable of succeeding.

Developing a healthy mental approach to test taking will also aid in other areas of life. Test anxiety affects more than just the actual test—it can be damaging to your mental health and even contribute to depression. It's important to beat test anxiety before it becomes a problem for more than testing.

Study Strategy

Being prepared for the test is necessary to combat anxiety, but what does being prepared look like? You may study for hours on end and still not feel prepared. What you need is a strategy for test prep. The next few pages outline our recommended steps to help you plan out and conquer the challenge of preparation.

Step 1: Scope Out the Test

Learn everything you can about the format (multiple choice, essay, etc.) and what will be on the test. Gather any study materials, course outlines, or sample exams that may be available. Not only will this help you to prepare, but knowing what to expect can help to alleviate test anxiety.

Step 2: Map Out the Material

Look through the textbook or study guide and make note of how many chapters or sections it has. Then divide these over the time you have. For example, if a book has 15 chapters and you have five days to study, you need to cover three chapters each day. Even better, if you have the time, leave an extra day at the end for overall review after you have gone through the material in depth.

If time is limited, you may need to prioritize the material. Look through it and make note of which sections you think you already have a good grasp on, and which need review. While you are studying, skim quickly through the familiar sections and take more time on the challenging parts.

Write out your plan so you don't get lost as you go. Having a written plan also helps you feel more in control of the study, so anxiety is less likely to arise from feeling overwhelmed at the amount to cover.

Step 3: Gather Your Tools

Decide what study method works best for you. Do you prefer to highlight in the book as you study and then go back over the highlighted portions? Or do you type out notes of the important information? Or is it helpful to make flashcards that you can carry with you? Assemble the pens, index cards, highlighters, post-it notes, and any other materials you may need so you won't be distracted by getting up to find things while you study.

If you're having a hard time retaining the information or organizing your notes, experiment with different methods. For example, try color-coding by subject with colored pens, highlighters, or post-it notes. If you learn better by hearing, try recording yourself reading your notes so you can listen while in the car, working out, or simply sitting at your desk. Ask a friend to quiz you from your flashcards, or try teaching someone the material to solidify it in your mind.

Step 4: Create Your Environment

It's important to avoid distractions while you study. This includes both the obvious distractions like visitors and the subtle distractions like an uncomfortable chair (or a too-comfortable couch that makes you want to fall asleep). Set up the best study environment possible: good lighting and a comfortable work area. If background music helps you focus, you may want to turn it on, but otherwise keep the room quiet. If you are using a computer to take notes, be sure you don't have any other windows open, especially applications like social media, games, or anything else that could distract you. Silence your phone and turn off notifications. Be sure to keep water close by so you stay hydrated while you study (but avoid unhealthy drinks and snacks).

Also, take into account the best time of day to study. Are you freshest first thing in the morning? Try to set aside some time then to work through the material. Is your mind clearer in the afternoon or evening? Schedule your study session then. Another method is to study at the same time of day that you will take the test, so that your brain gets used to working on the material at that time and will be ready to focus at test time.

Step 5: Study!

Once you have done all the study preparation, it's time to settle into the actual studying. Sit down, take a few moments to settle your mind so you can focus, and begin to follow your study plan. Don't give in to distractions or let yourself procrastinate. This is your time to prepare so you'll be ready to fearlessly approach the test. Make the most of the time and stay focused.

Of course, you don't want to burn out. If you study too long you may find that you're not retaining the information very well. Take regular study breaks. For example, taking five minutes out of every hour to walk briskly, breathing deeply and swinging your arms, can help your mind stay fresh.

As you get to the end of each chapter or section, it's a good idea to do a quick review. Remind yourself of what you learned and work on any difficult parts. When you feel that you've mastered the material, move on to the next part. At the end of your study session, briefly skim through your notes again.

But while review is helpful, cramming last minute is NOT. If at all possible, work ahead so that you won't need to fit all your study into the last day. Cramming overloads your brain with more information than it can process and retain, and your tired mind may struggle to recall even previously learned information when it is overwhelmed with last-minute study. Also, the urgent nature of cramming and the stress placed on your brain contribute to anxiety. You'll be more likely to go to the test feeling unprepared and having trouble thinking clearly.

So don't cram, and don't stay up late before the test, even just to review your notes at a leisurely pace. Your brain needs rest more than it needs to go over the information again. In fact, plan to finish your studies by noon or early afternoon the day before the test. Give your brain the rest of the day to relax or focus on other things, and get a good night's sleep. Then you will be fresh for the test and better able to recall what you've studied.

Step 6: Take a Practice Test

Many courses offer sample tests, either online or in the study materials. This is an excellent resource to check whether you have mastered the material, as well as to prepare for the test format and environment.

Check the test format ahead of time: the number of questions, the type (multiple choice, free response, etc.), and the time limit. Then create a plan for working through them. For example, if you have 30 minutes to take a 60-question test, your limit is 30 seconds per question. Spend less time on the questions you know well so that you can take more time on the difficult ones.

If you have time to take several practice tests, take the first one open book, with no time limit. Work through the questions at your own pace and make sure you fully understand them. Gradually work up to taking a test under test conditions: sit at a desk with all study materials put away and set a timer. Pace yourself to make sure you finish the test with time to spare and go back to check your answers if you have time.

After each test, check your answers. On the questions you missed, be sure you understand why you missed them. Did you misread the question (tests can use tricky wording)? Did you forget the information? Or was it something you hadn't learned? Go back and study any shaky areas that the practice tests reveal.

Taking these tests not only helps with your grade, but also aids in combating test anxiety. If you're already used to the test conditions, you're less likely to worry about it, and working through tests until you're scoring well gives you a confidence boost. Go through the practice tests until you feel comfortable, and then you can go into the test knowing that you're ready for it.

Test Tips

On test day, you should be confident, knowing that you've prepared well and are ready to answer the questions. But aside from preparation, there are several test day strategies you can employ to maximize your performance.

First, as stated before, get a good night's sleep the night before the test (and for several nights before that, if possible). Go into the test with a fresh, alert mind rather than staying up late to study.

Try not to change too much about your normal routine on the day of the test. It's important to eat a nutritious breakfast, but if you normally don't eat breakfast at all, consider eating just a protein bar. If you're a coffee drinker, go ahead and have your normal coffee. Just make sure you time it so that the caffeine doesn't wear off right in the middle of your test. Avoid sugary beverages, and drink enough water to stay hydrated but not so much that you need a restroom break 10 minutes into the test. If your test isn't first thing in the morning, consider going for a walk or doing a light workout before the test to get your blood flowing.

Allow yourself enough time to get ready, and leave for the test with plenty of time to spare so you won't have the anxiety of scrambling to arrive in time. Another reason to be early is to select a good seat. It's helpful to sit away from doors and windows, which can be distracting. Find a good seat, get out your supplies, and settle your mind before the test begins.

When the test begins, start by going over the instructions carefully, even if you already know what to expect. Make sure you avoid any careless mistakes by following the directions.

Then begin working through the questions, pacing yourself as you've practiced. If you're not sure on an answer, don't spend too much time on it, and don't let it shake your confidence. Either skip it and come back later, or eliminate as many wrong answers as possible and guess among the remaining ones. Don't dwell on these questions as you continue—put them out of your mind and focus on what lies ahead.

Be sure to read all of the answer choices, even if you're sure the first one is the right answer. Sometimes you'll find a better one if you keep reading. But don't second-guess yourself if you do immediately know the answer. Your gut instinct is usually right. Don't let test anxiety rob you of the information you know.

If you have time at the end of the test (and if the test format allows), go back and review your answers. Be cautious about changing any, since your first instinct tends to be correct, but make sure you didn't misread any of the questions or accidentally mark the wrong answer choice. Look over any you skipped and make an educated guess.

At the end, leave the test feeling confident. You've done your best, so don't waste time worrying about your performance or wishing you could change anything. Instead, celebrate the successful completion of this test. And finally, use this test to learn how to deal with anxiety even better next time.

Review Video: Test Anxiety
Visit mometrix.com/academy and enter code: 100340

Important Qualification

Not all anxiety is created equal. If your test anxiety is causing major issues in your life beyond the classroom or testing center, or if you are experiencing troubling physical symptoms related to your anxiety, it may be a sign of a serious physiological or psychological condition. If this sounds like your situation, we strongly encourage you to seek professional help.

Online Resources

Due to our efforts to try to keep this book to a manageable length, we've created a link that will give you access to all of your online resources:

mometrix.com/resources719/abcteworldhist

It's Your Moment, Let's Celebrate It!

Share your story @mometrixtestpreparation